Bone of My Bones

Bone of My Bones

Cynthia Gaw

RESOURCE *Publications* • Eugene, Oregon

BONE OF MY BONES

Copyright © 2015 Cynthia Gaw. All rights reserved. Except for brief quotations in critical publications or reviews, no part of this book may be reproduced in any manner without prior written permission from the publisher. Write: Permissions. Wipf and Stock Publishers, 199 W. 8th Ave., Suite 3, Eugene, OR 97401.

Resource Publications
An Imprint of Wipf and Stock Publishers
199 W. 8th Ave., Suite 3
Eugene, OR 97401

www.wipfandstock.com

ISBN 13: 978-1-4982-2552-6

Manufactured in the U.S.A.   10/02/2015

Dedicated to the loving memory of our son
August Skye
and to the shalom of
Sara Marie and Hunter Skye

Author's Note

AT THE COMMENCEMENT OF this book I stand upon a very strong and stable bridge about to jump into a whitewater of controversy. The conversation into which I plunge rages. But because those whom I seek to persuade share the bridge, I believe agreement is possible. We have so much common ground. We share a high view of the Bible as our final authority and a common set of hermeneutical principles by which to interpret that inerrant revelation. We share the same Savior, Spirit, and Father to lead us into truth and model for us relational perfection. We are all organic, essential organs of the same holy, catholic and apostolic body of Christ on earth. And we all know that our God has chosen to edify us through that community. We trust alone in Christ for our salvation, so unity will eventually be perfected in him. We share the knowledge of our finite and sinful natures which obliges us to humility in the face of infinite truth; we, none of us, have perfect understanding and are, therefore, needing to hear the understandings of our brothers and sisters in Christ that the transformation of our minds may progress. For this purpose we need those who disagree with us more than those who agree. These brothers and sisters will, however, do us little good if we do not listen, and really hear, what they say. The authority and truth of the Word of God is not threatened by a human misunderstanding or blind spot. But transformations in our thinking which are consistent with that Word prove it powerful and efficacious.

Those I seek to persuade not only share a firm foundation, but also important conclusions on our subject. Equality of essence is not denied by any of us. We agree that monogamous, heterosexual marriage is prescriptive and good. We agree that gender diversity is complementary. We agree that service to God and others from a motive of love is not demeaning, but a positive act of freedom and an enlargement of the human personality. We agree that nurturing and training children happens best within a loving family and that it is a high calling for both genders. We agree that temporary, gift and talent-based hierarchies are sometimes wise. The point of disagreement I address is that the Scriptures teach a gender-based hierarchy within the church and family.

I have declined to write an academic book on the subject because it simply is not needed. All necessary research has been done and written up. So I have chosen fiction, a genre not true to facts, but true to both ideas and experience. The university campus setting is my world, in that sense only is the following narrative autobiographical. I speak only of my experience. All characters are fiction.

Prologue

To the woman he said, "I will make your pains in childbearing very severe; with painful labor you will give birth to children. Your desire will be for your husband, and he will rule over you."

—Genesis 3:16

Drew came in through the walkout basement door of a fraternity house on Clement Street. He knew the guy sitting at the little Formica table was not a student, and that his name was not "Joe"; but he had been highly recommended by his older brother, John, who was experienced in these matters. A quick glance told Drew that "Joe" had all things necessary in this basement. A locked built-in cabinet, a shelf with unused steel-wool and an unopened box of sandpaper sitting next to a well-used can of paint stripper, a Victorian dining chair needing refinishing, and an old laundry sink completed the scene. The odd tools, camping equipment, tennis rackets, golf clubs, and many pieces of luggage held their obvious and legitimate place in storage. Drew sat down at the table across from Joe and pulled out his wallet.

Joe said, "My work is guaranteed, but your girlfriends must be between one hundred twenty and one hundred fifty pounds. Make sure they are 'good girls' with absolutely no alcohol or drugs onboard. Mix this with two quarts of orange juice and two quarts of 7-Up, both cold. Float some lemon slices for insurance. Fifteen minutes from consuming four ounces of the substance, they are yours. Unconsciousness is possible between twenty and thirty minutes, but they will come back about forty minutes from consumption. Return them to the place of consumption by that time. By forty-five minutes they will be with it, but not feeling all that great. You hope they want to go home and take a nap. For if they fall asleep, they won't wake up until past time for detection in urine." Drew handed Joe four crisp one hundred dollar bills. Joe handed Drew a bottle like one he had seen many times in the "Colds" section at his pharmacy. It read "Sterile Saline

Nasal Relief Spray." In smaller lettering, he saw "Clears Congestion without Medicine." Drew left the basement less than two minutes from entering it with the distilled curse in his hand.

Chapter 1

There is neither Jew nor Gentile, neither slave nor free, nor is there male and female, for you are all one in Christ Jesus.

—Galatians 3:28

She felt she achieved an insight into her new culture when Nora learned that the largest bookstore in Poplar was Firm Foundation Christian Books. The fact related to the astonishing number of Baptist churches in the small town coexisting with almost every other denomination she knew. She pulled into its generous parking lot from the main highway coming into town from the south. It was situated in her least favorite part of town, where the box stores and fast food chains congregated, and where pedestrians were practically prohibited. Cyclists who shopped in the area constantly risked serious bodily harm. The surroundings contrasted with the old downtown she and Luke so enjoyed. Firm Foundation comfortably neighbored a Walmart big box on one side and a Lowe's home improvement store on the other.

She was here because the moving van was missing an important box when it arrived in Poplar. The most difficult decisions in the moving process had been about books. The library was the heart of their old home and the room in which they spent the most time. It had floor-to-ceiling, built-in bookcases on three walls and both their desks on the other. The new house had only two small bookcases, and the moving company charged by the pound. Books aren't light. Nora's extensive collection of children's literature was divided up for the grandchildren, and only the most useful and important of the other volumes had been boxed to bring across the country. She had missed the box marked "Bible Reference" even before the movers left. Their inventory checklist confirmed her disappointment. The box next to item #267 was not ticked, and the truck was empty. Today's errand was to estimate the cost of replacing item #267, but it was not replaceable. Her Strong's concordance, for example, had been given to her by her father, and its copious marginal notes begun when she was thirteen years old. Her Kittel's New Testament dictionary was safely on the shelf in the new house because those ten volumes had filled a box of their own. She always found it difficult to consider her New Testament dictionary, especially when she had Galatians 3:28 on the back burner. Here was a brilliant man and a great scholar of the New Testament who could interpret Paul's letter to the Galatians *and* enthusiastically and anti-Semitically support the Nazis. The text had not been the problem, but the cultural blind spot of the man. Dr. Schaeffer had several times reminded her that all of us have blind spots that we bring to the Scripture. But Nora prayed with all her heart that God would make her a Bonhoeffer—not a Kittel.

She missed the *Keyword Study Bible* that Luke had given her soon after Blythe was born, her old Greek and Hebrew Lexicons, and other basic tools. Hmmm . . . maybe she should start doing even more research online? Others felt they saved time, but she didn't think she could. The lost books were places, not digital spaces, where she could immediately find what she needed. Books didn't get viruses or glitches. They didn't bombard one with advertising in the privacy of one's own desk. One only had to learn to use them once. They didn't suddenly disappear for a mysterious reason. She was very thankful for the convenience and vastness of the private academic databases on the library website, but she loved her books more. Why did she feel the loss of her books so much when research experiences in cyberspace were open to her? After all, her books could disappear from a moving van. Perhaps she was the technological stick-in-the-mud her children thought her?

Looking through her windshield, Nora explored her ambivalence to entering the store as she looked at the facade. It was a well-designed, timber frame, three-story, mountain style building with beautiful stonework, huge timbers and three-story-high open beams. Why didn't she like going to these places? It contained many expressions of the gospel she loved. It encouraged and supported many local churches and promoted worship, concepts dear to her heart.

American culture seemed always to press faith into an isolated cubby entitled "Religion," and this business, perhaps because it was a business, seemed to challenge that marginalization. If one's child had been asking for a new puzzle, one might choose one of Jonah and the whale or Noah's ark rather than SpongeBob Square Pants or a Disney character. The choice itself seemed to break down barriers between faith and daily life. Nevertheless, she knew the feeling of rejection she was likely to encounter. She

Chapter 1

anticipated that old feeling of being out of sync with the church, of somehow not belonging properly to Christ's body, indeed, of not being seen as fully human.

Sure, there were cultural gaps. The store was far too upscale to reconcile with the poor church she loved in Kenya. It was too open for the persecuted church she loved in Uzbekistan. It was too individualistic for the liturgy and High-Church aesthetics she loved when she was working on her PhD in the Church of Wales. And no city the size of Poplar in Western Europe could financially support such a business with their tiny percentage of evangelical Christians. The irrelevance reached far deeper. For in these sorts of expressions of Christianity, she always felt rejected for who she was. She foresaw the oncoming dissonance between her identity and her spiritual community. She prepared herself for the nice, passive, silent onslaught with Galatians 3:28.

Last week Nora had read another "complementarian" defend the passage from "those evangelical feminists" who used it as a "panacea." But the argument had seemed hopelessly weak. The more she studied the passage in context, the better it made her feel—nobody could deny that. It seemed to Nora a clarion call to unity with profoundly panacean tendencies, indeed, a cultural cure-all. She was a female person united to Christ, and that qualified her to claim the promises in the text and establish her unique place in the body of Christ. Something else about the passage could not be denied, and that was that it was a parallelism. Whatever the nature of the differences in the classes of people and its divisiveness in the church, it was the same for Jews and Gentiles, people on the low and high ends of the socioeconomic ladder, and men and women. If it was clearly wrong for one antonymic class of people, it would be wrong for all three. And if it was right for a contrasting class, it would be right for the other two.

After four more recitations of Galatians 3:28, she exited the four-wheeled confines of her personal space, clicked the padlock icon on her Subaru key, and entered the zeitgeist of Contemporary American Christianity and one milieu of her faith.

The dramatic wood and glass doors opened automatically into a three-story foyer toward the back of which ran a U-shaped service counter with several clerk stations. A broad oaken double staircase rose to the second floor from behind the counter. A middle-aged woman with excellent taste in clothes and make-up, greeted her with a friendly, "Good morning, may I help you find anything?"

"Perhaps you could point the way to your reference section?" asked Nora as she pulled a clipboard out of her backpack.

"Reference works are on the third floor at the back of the store. Another associate is up there. There is an elevator there if you prefer." She motioned to an alcove behind and under the staircase.

Nora headed up the stairs with a simple, "Thank you."

On her way up the stairs she noticed that the large room to the right of the foyer with many rows of stacks had a sign above its entrance that said, "Women." So, when she got to the back of the third floor, she looked for a sign of the same design that said, "Bible Reference."

Expecting a sign over the top of the doorway like "Women," a few minutes passed before she found her objective. The sign was waist high because the reference section only covered the bottom three shelves of the small stack. Nora sighed with disappointment and stared at the miniscule collection. She sat down on the floor to see the one shelf of interest to her—the bottom shelf. Next to some Unger's handbooks and dictionaries, she saw *The New Strong's Concordance with Vine's Dictionary*. As she was reaching for it, she heard steps approaching. They came to a halt beside her. She looked up. A tall, lean man of indeterminate middle age smiled down at her from above his clerical collar. But when he looked at the sign and its corresponding works, his smile fell off. "Oh, dear, I was expecting a better selection—it's such a large store. This is rather scanty."

Nora felt the tug of personal connection and agreed, "Positively meager."

"Well," he replied, "I need the new edition of *The Oxford Encyclopedia of the Books of the Bible*, but apparently my choice is between Amazon, for which I'll need to wait a week, and an e-book, which will have no friendly pages to turn . . . Oh, I see you're thinking about the new Strong's; I highly recommend it. Having Vine's dictionary in the same volume is rather convenient."

"We just lost a box of reference books in a move; this will replace two birds with one stone," she remarked.

"Oh, dear," he said with a genuine note of sympathy. "That would be a hard loss. My family and I also recently moved here, but without a serious mishap. Everything arrived, and only some trifles weren't in one piece. What's a thrift store crock pot and an old lamp compared to a concordance?"

Nora chuckled and asked herself why she had been so reluctant to enter this store. "Do you serve a church here in Poplar?" she asked.

Chapter 1

"I do."

"Are you a Catholic priest?"

"Wrong," he said with a grin. "Guess again."

"A Lutheran?" came the next query.

"No, I am an Anglican pastor."

"Really, my husband and I have been looking for a church, and we hadn't noticed that there was an Anglican church in Poplar. Are you with St. Mark's Episcopal?"

"No, we're a bit more on the conservative side of the theological spectrum than our brothers and sisters at St. Mark's. I serve at King of Kings. We are a small church family without a building of our own. We meet in a hotel conference room, a La Quinta sanctuary, you might say. I'm Cormac Bruce, by the way, pleased to meet you."

"I'm Nora Shaw," she said as they shook hands.

"Oh, dear," he exclaimed looking at his watch in a way that suggested he didn't have a gift for administration, "My son needs picking up from his piano lesson . . . Should you and your husband be inclined to visit us at King of Kings, we'd all be delighted." He pulled his wallet from his hip pocket and removed a business-sized card. "Godspeed," was his valediction as he handed it to her. "I hope we meet again soon."

As his step descended the stairs, she looked down at the card in her hand and smiled at the familiar blue shield with its red cross, the white star in each quadrant, and the miter in the middle. "I think we will," she thought.

Descending the open staircase she could see the whole store.

A gift section dominated by visual arts was the largest. Framed prints, yard art, t-shirts, jewelry, mugs, and knickknacks of every imaginable sort were displayed by an employee with sound marketing background. To Nora the art reflected the popular culture more than Christianity, yet it seemed to insulate a Christian subculture all the more. She didn't see any objects with power to transform or enrich the culture. None of the prints were by Rembrandt or Albrecht Dürer. There were some beautiful photographs of the local Blue Ridge Mountains; apparently God's creation could speak for itself. But the selection was predominantly a display of kitsch to catch the consumer.

She thought of the young artist Beatrice Edgars, who she and Luke had met last week. Her faith organically and intentionally informed her aesthetic theory and her paintings; her gallery in Blowing Rock was doing very well. But her prints would look displaced in this predictable and insipid assemblage. Car art was one genre particularly well-represented. Gnomic biblical quotations accustomed to incisive alteration of the human heart leaked power when printed on a piece of vinyl adhesive. Wisdom literature did not translate well into a five-dollar advertising slogan on a bumper sticker. One could imagine it being efficacious only in the worst of traffic jams; usually it would just lose meaning from overuse.

The children's section was large, but again merely a cultural mirror. She saw a display of Veggie Tales lunch boxes, a shelf of Fun With Jesus water guns, and a stack of God Is Awesome stationery sets, good perhaps for making a hit at a birthday party—but not particularly productive of spiritual growth. Indeed, the stock appeared to promote identification with commercial products rather than with Jesus. The business model merged ecumenism and retail marketing, culturally specific Christianity and capitalism—not wrong perhaps, but at least uneasy bedfellows.

The greeting card section occupied at least fifty feet of wall space. Above the cards, higher than the reach of the human hand, was a large print in a thick, antique gold frame. In the center of the scene, a lovely thatched cottage radiated a deep golden light. Every flower in its idyllic English garden was visible although it was night. The vignette exhibited the baptism of Hallmark officiated by the sentimentalism of Thomas Kincaid. Was that irresistible light sourced by the love of Christ or an "Angel in the House"? If she hadn't been so sinful, would the Holy Spirit have produced such a paradise for her family? She didn't know, but she felt certain that the people who lived in the painted cottage could not possibly understand the losses she and Luke had endured together.

With a sudden inspiration and a prayer for emotional courage, Nora decided to take an alphabetic cruise through the "Women's" stacks.

In the B's Nora picked up *8 Choices That Will Change a Woman's Life* by Jill Briscoe. Scanning the table of contents did, indeed, reveal eight important choices: To resist pain or to use it; To gather wealth or to gather grace; To speak wisely or to speak foolishly; To value our time or to fritter it away; To live for ourselves or to live for the Spirit; To develop God's gifts or to waste them; To persevere or to protest; To stand for truth or to abandon it. Nora concluded that the only problem was the title, which should be *8 Choices That Will Change Anybody's Life*.

Cheryl Brodersen's *When a Woman Chooses to Forgive* brought to Nora's mind the questions "How do the consequences of forgiveness vary according to the gender of the forgiver?" and "How does the choice to forgive impact the character of men and women differently?" She also recognized her own stupid questions.

The full shelf of Larry Crabb's *Fully Alive* was highlighted by a special sign. Here was indeed a curiosity of staggering import. On his first page of part 1, Crabb insists upon gender *before* humanity, upending the hierarchy of biblical Christianity from its inception. Nora was flabbergasted. She had always thought that "male" and "female" were adjectives qualifying a species noun like "human being" or "dog"—that the substantive governed the modifier. She had interpreted from Genesis that all human beings created in the image of God held a unique place in the great chain of being and had profound dignity, only "a little lower than the angels"—then that human beings were either male or female. But this was flatly denied by Crabb. "Femininity or masculinity is so irrevocably and irreversibly embedded in our being that no one can accurately say, 'I am first a person and then male or female.'"[1] Nora reasoned, "So I have more in common with Lassie because she's female than with my husband who's only another human being. Crabb has rejected the basis for social justice and human rights in the West in a single flippant claim. Perhaps Frederick Douglass should have argued for the abolition of slavery on the basis of his masculinity? He would not then have needed to support women's rights to maintain his logical consistency. Crabb has made dehumanization a goal, not an evil."

Nora thought how "feminine" refers us to our human nature, while "godly" refers us to our full humanity as his image bearers. We, both women and men, are to establish our identity in Christ. We ought to desire to conform to his character not to some relative definition of femininity. Crabb has produced no biblical definition of "femininity"; the word does not appear in the Bible. Nora stopped to take a few deep breaths, but continued to fall into her Galatians 3:28 mantra.

When she began to surface, she was surprised by a lonely copy of J. Lee Grady's *10 Mentiras que la Iglesia Le Dice a las Mujeres*, and a nod at honesty. English speakers in Poplar were not given the exposure of the lies. But the little book's appearance on the shelf suggested to the very observant shopper that other cultures might be attempting to get to the truth.

In the H's *How to Get the Best Out of Your Man: The Power of a Woman's Influence* by Hammond smacked of manipulation and the objectification of both sexes.

---

1. Crabb, *Fully Alive*, 21.

Sixteen titles by Sharon Jaynes lined the shelves. All contained precise definitions of gender, the feminine role, and a tightly delineated sphere for the sisters.

Le Roux and Douglas's *Promises from God for Women* was bound in elegant pink leather, inscribed with a floral design (Christian Art Gifts, 2003). The only things not stereotypically feminine were the Bible passages, which were equally applicable to men.

Several titles by Stormie Omartian had prominent place, but most copies were *The Power of the Praying Wife* and *The Power of the Praying Woman*. Nora thought, "If the power comes from God, wouldn't the power of a praying husband and a praying man be similar? Or do females pray differently than other people?"

In the P's two feet of shelf space was filled with Piper and Grudem's *Recovering Biblical Manhood & Womanhood*, but not a single copy of Pierce and Groothuis's superior *Discovering Biblical Equality* was to be seen.

In the R's she came across Jerry Richards's *Day Break Verses for Women*. Nora loved Matins. But as she thought back through her long experience with them, she couldn't remember any verses specifically aimed at women. Perhaps the strongest female voice traditionally used in the morning was Mary's *Magnificat*. But that song, as much as any in the Bible, was the corporate voice of the whole church. It was men and women as humble brides responding to the divine lover. Nora thought of males all over the world joyfully declaring themselves "handmaidens," without any threat to their masculinity.

This whole section of the store rightly emphasized hidden, quiet, humble service. But Nora noted nothing in the T's by Teresa of Calcutta.

Lysa TerKeurst's books all prompted a tagline: *What Happens When Women Say Yes to God* prompted "the same as when men say yes to God"; *What Happens When Women Walk in Faith*, "the same as when men walk in faith"; the gerund-phrase title *Becoming More Than a Good Bible Study Girl*, "the same as becoming more than a good Bible study boy."

This section of the store, more than any other, completely lacked historical perspective. Not a single work written before the 1970s was displayed. The voice of Christian women through the centuries was utterly ignored. Not a single copy of Aelia Eudocia, Radegund, Hrotsvitha, Marie de France, Beatrice of Nazareth, Catherine of Sienna, Julian of Norwich, Hildegard of Bingen, Christine de Pizan, Teresa de Cartagena, or Teresa of Avila showed itself. Nora thought, "Wouldn't it be refreshing to see just

CHAPTER 1

a slim little volume containing a modern translation of Chaucer's 'Wife of Bath's Prologue and Tale' sitting among this monopoly on gender concepts?" Alison could, with a single toss of Jankyn's book into the fire, solve many of the problems these popular books address, and more importantly expose biblical truth. Her comedy, experience and plain sense affirm marriage and women more than a truckload of this stuff.

Nora looked back to the H's for a serious attempt to establish the status quo of these stacks with biblical scholarship. But no, not even an influential champion of their own before 1985, like James B. Hurley's *Man and Woman in Biblical Perspective*, was represented. Strange, thought Nora, that the "complementarian" position that separates equality of essence from equality of function should so often be referred to as the "traditional" view, for it is so utterly brand new.

Chapter 2

Receive my instruction, and not silver,
And knowledge rather than choice gold;
For wisdom is better than rubies,
And all the things one may desire cannot be compared with her.

—Proverbs 8:10–11

Having proven many times the stereotype of the absentminded professor by walking into someone else's assembled classroom, Dr. Shaw checks her watch—almost ten o'clock, and the number on the door—206. She then pauses just a moment to invoke her heavenly teaching muse. "Please give me good questions; make me quick to ask and slow to tell."

At 9:55 the Avery halls surge with the between-lecture swarms, the hive ashift. In six minutes those halls will be almost deserted, filled only with a distant buzz of merged professorial voices.

The classroom is about half full. The teacher sees the active, worker-students tuck into their desk-shaped cells poised to produce sweet knowledge, wisdom, and truth. The professor queen produces a variety of pheromone assignments, lectures, and discussions that regulate the behavior of the workers. But the workers choose her, and she is there only to serve their need for intellectual fertility; they generally respect and appreciate her for her service to them.

But occasionally, somewhere in the comb of desks, a passive, stingless drone-student merely occupies his or her waxen nest. These students serve the queen only, nothing higher, and that with as little work as possible. They have no function apart from service to her, and the queen is, therefore, always a tyrant to them. Believing grade A honey will fill them through the action of the queen, they idly avoid the discipline and thought that produce grade A honey, and consequently live in a perpetual and anxious state of cognitive dissonance. Wanting only the A and doing little to earn it, passive

Chapter 2

students have no joy in the relational or educational process and become mere desk-warmers, place-takers in an impersonal social system of geometrical purposelessness, grinding out an almost meaningless degree.

Workers serve the community in diverse ways according to many specializations and gifts; they ask interesting questions as they seek to bring the ideas in great literature to bear upon their own lives and understanding; they look for relevance and connections; they are drawn into conversation and relationships with peers and professors; their vast differences in background and personal temperament enrich their classrooms and turn those classrooms into microcosms of society. Workers believe in the existence of a state called ignorance which they want to avoid and in the existence, however nebulous, of a quality called wisdom which they want to absorb.

Drones are haploid, male only, unifunctional. Drones are careful never to learn anything that won't be on the exam. They willingly accept an impersonal place in the educational mill and don't mind becoming, with their degree, ground-out products for sale. Drones come to a university only to get prepared to earn a living in a way that deconstructs the abundant life. Lucky for the hive that workers far outnumber drones.

Nora Shaw opens her backpack, pulls out a stack of thirty-five reading quizzes on the Sumerian myth *The Descent of Inanna*, lays them on the table at the front of the classroom, and announces, "You may begin your quiz when you are ready to close your textbook." The workers realize she's giving them fifteen minutes to take a ten-minute quiz. They have extra time to think and craft articulate answers. They thankfully smile as they come forward to pick up their quizzes. Drones are always irritated when a professor begins before the top of the hour. The two drones see, but cannot hear, what is happening and keep their earbuds in.

At 10:04, breathless and sweaty from the jog from Walker Hall, Jason Critcher quietly slips into a desk near the door. The worker bee meets the queen's eye with a genuine apologetic smile; she returns the smile with one of her own that reassures him that the tardy will not be recorded. She thinks, "The administration is correct; the hike from fourth-floor Walker to second-floor Avery can be made in ten minutes, but barely. If one has a long-winded calculus professor and both a calculus textbook and a world lit anthology in one's backpack, it cannot be done."

At 10:07, Andrew Mitchell, who asked to be called Drew, strolls casually and confidently across the front of the class, and takes a seat on the far side with a very polite and very disruptive greeting. The queen feels an undercurrent of disrespect in the drone's surface chivalry. His tidy loafers, creased khakis, and buttoned-down collar do not bespeak hurry. As he sits down, he looks the queen squarely in the eye. She sees arrogant challenge rather than apology.

She ponders, "How does one write an attendance policy in a syllabus for Jasons and Andrews?" The usual strategy crafts a strict policy to protect the administration and the professor from the complaints of drones and then ignores the policy in the majority cases of cooperative workers. All students then note the irrelevance of the syllabus and don't bother to read it. Getting a new syllabus is like getting an owner's manual with a new hair dryer. One plugs it in and turns it on, not needing to read again that "electrical appliances should not be submerged or the plastic bags they come in slipped over the heads of toddlers." It is only given to protect the manufacturer, not to help the user. Getting students to read the helpful parts of a syllabus is like a flight attendant getting passengers to "pay close attention" to their four thousandth lesson on how to buckle a seat belt. One is simply tuned out.

At 10:10 Dr. Shaw directs the class to "please pass your quiz to a classmate and pull out your green pen for editing." Amid the now-rustling class, Rachel and Crystal exchange papers and rummage in backpacks for a green pen. Rachel is a nursing major who told her professor during an office visit that she wants to work in a developing country with a missionary organization. She is one of two very dissimilar homeschooled students in that section of ancient world lit. Although well-prepared for university work in terms of knowledge, Dr. Shaw suspects her imagination is semi-dormant and her critical sense unexercised. The professor thinks her family must be of the "Christ-against culture" mindset in which holiness means to retreat from the world and to circle the wagons in self-defense, rather than to go forth as salt and light into the world. Her demeanor is confident and her countenance open, but a yawning chasm exists between her and even her Christian women classmates. Her modest, comfortable jean skirt, long simple hairstyle, and cotton-print blouse advertise an utter indifference to fashion from which the more fashionable Christian girls seek to distance themselves. The professor approves her desire to live in a developing culture, for she is relationally handicapped in her own. In the mountains of Ecuador or the highlands of Kenya, nobody will notice she is clueless of her own culture, and her concern for them will prompt her to learn about their culture. Dr. Shaw especially likes Rachel and sees the potential that this course has to enrich her intellectual life.

Chapter 2

If only Crystal had some of Rachel's indifference to pop culture and some of her self-confidence. Crystal is poured into jeans two sizes too small. Some of her extra pounds billow out in the broad gap between her hip-huggers and the bottom of her tight tank top. To her teacher, Crystal seems desperate to conform to worldly expectations that are, according to Jean Kilbourne, "killing her softly." Her immodesty advertises her need to be attractive to men. Her identity seems dominated by her sexual appeal. Dr. Shaw hopes the literature will draw Crystal, who is a worker, into new interests. Servat Kalpar, who sits next to Crystal, sympathizes with her classmate from inside her hijab; "These poor, loose American women have lost their self-respect."

Servat is a pre-med student from Pakistan. Her first language is Urdu, and her exposure to literature very limited, so this course will be a major challenge for her. Servat is worried, but not her professor. Dr. Shaw recognizes a diligent and serious student when she sees one, and she knows that Servat will be in her office when she needs the help she's been sincerely offered. The A expected in her science classes isn't likely, but this active worker will no doubt buzz past a C.

Servat acquired her student visa with her uncle's help. Rasheed Uncle is a professor in the medical school at Chapel Hill, and he advised her father that her application at his medical school would be strong with good grades from Blue Ridge. She knows her father in Multan considers a Pakistani medical doctor trained in America the best hope for her future, and that her father will accept her uncle's advice on a suitable husband. So, even though Servat has never met her father's brother, she sees Rasheed Uncle as controlling her future. She plans to stay with her uncle's family in Chapel Hill over Thanksgiving break, and she's nervous about the visit. Servat wisely traded quizzes with Theodore Mullins, whose editing comments will be concise and helpful.

Nora Shaw knew she had one of the best students of her career when Theodore Mullins came into her office on the second day of the semester. He was the other homeschooled student, but of the "Christ transformer of culture" variety. It wasn't just that he had already read some of the works on the syllabus, but that he had heard of most of them and felt left out of conversations he wanted to be a part of because he had not read them all. From the few questions she had asked him about his background, she determined that Dorothy Sayers' lost tools of learning had been not only recovered, but sharpened and used extensively. Even his first reading quiz reflected deep understanding of classical logic and rhetoric. His vastly superior academic background had produced no recognizable hubris. He was curious and qualified, humble and eager. She sensed in him a commitment to the truth that would make him one of the few students courageous enough to exemplify the definition of a good student that she and Donald Drew had hammered out over tea so many years ago. She went over that definition in her mind applying it to Theodore, or Ted as he asked to be called.

He had sound reasons for being in school and a worthy motive for study coupled with a capacity for self-discipline and accuracy in thought and methods. He did not confuse excellence with elitism. He was not necessarily possessed of a high IQ (although she suspected Ted's was sky high), but he did have the inclination and the will to sit down in a library and apply himself to difficult studies. He studied the influential people of history, in their original writings or as close to that as possible, and did not parrot slogans he thought that person might have said. He examined reality with integrity. He followed an argument where it led, accepted evidence for what it was worth, and took imaginative leaps, but not beyond the strict barrier of truth. This was a young man who would productively use what others have written as a springboard to dive into the sea of his own ideas. He did not dissent without understanding what he was challenging. He was utterly indifferent to intellectual popularity or fashion, and he inflexibly denied that truth was decided by counting votes. Deep down he knew that his education did not stop off campus, but continued all day and throughout his lifetime. He was aware that he would gradually develop growth in understanding. Dr. Shaw sensed he would never lose his sense of wonder, and that he was aware of his own humble but significant place in God's purposes.

Ted was one of her few local students. He grew up in a large extended family on a mountain in nearby Cross Valley. The professor and her husband, Luke, had visited a church called Poplar Bible Fellowship where she had heard of the extended family. After his home-high school, Ted wasn't sure what he should study or where he should study it. So he and his old grandmother decided that he would live at home, study a year at Blue Ridge for minimal expense and major in philosophy for broad background. Ted rode to campus from Mullins Mountain with his Uncle Hank, who taught in the computer science department.

Dana Blevin traded quizzes with Andrea on his right. Dana's particularly tight low-riding jeans, unbuttoned yellow polo, stylish, slip-on Italian shoes, up-combed hair, and earring certainly had a gay look. Dana was an intelligent worker bee; Nora would have no trouble making him feel accepted. Some texts were friendly with homoeroticism; some were not. Gilgamesh and Enkidu came in early in the course and offered an opportunity for frank and respectful conversation on that subject. Dana was especially receptive to poetic language and artistic in temperament. He would be an outstanding student.

Matthew Okonkwo traded quizzes with Travis Williams, both of whom, Dr. Shaw knew, would bring a strong perspective to class conversation. Matthew was a towering basketball player from Edo State in Nigeria. He was in no danger of taking his opportunity at Blue Ridge for granted, for his athletic scholarship had most likely been his ticket out of extreme poverty. English was his fourth language, and his genius was on the court. Ancient literature would take work, but his profound thankfulness for just being where he was produced a respect, for the class, the professor, his classmates, and the subject, that made him extremely teachable.

Travis Williams would definitely add an important perspective to the class. He was a confident and outspoken atheist and an active member of the Freedom From Religion Foundation. Dr. Shaw had already noted the strong influence of Bertrand Russell and George Bernard Shaw upon Travis' thought. He was an evolutionary biology major with a reverence for Richard Dawkins. Ancient and medieval world literature looked continually at religions and worldviews. Travis would remind the class of the logical possibility that they may all be wrong.

Chapter 3

For the Lord your God is God of gods ...

—Deuteronomy 10:17

"... The temple of the great goddess Artemis may be despised and her magnificence destroyed, whom all Asia and the world worship." Now when they heard this, they were full of wrath and cried out, saying, "Great is Artemis of the Ephesians!" So the whole city was filled with confusion ...

—Acts 19:27–29

"I'll remind you, editors," said Dr. Shaw, "that I will grade the reading quizzes in red. You have the more important job of making marginal comments about how your classmate's answer could be improved. As you seriously try to help your classmate, you're helping yourself. It's a win/win; please edit carefully as we discuss."

Dr. Shaw began with her first question, "Jason, why do you think 'The Descent of Inanna' is our first reading assignment?"

"Because it's the oldest story," came the immediate reply.

"Is it?" asked the teacher.

"Well, it is the oldest literature. I guess it might not be the oldest story."

"How do you know that?"

"It's got lots of parts that repeat the same phrase over and over, and you can often see that it's following a formula. The book says that shows that whoever wrote the story down was working from an oral, traditional story that is much older."

"Good, Jason. Rachel, why is 'The Descent of Inanna' the oldest literature in our anthology?"

Rachel answered, "It was written in cuneiform on clay tablets, so it didn't rot."

Chapter 3

"Right, but what did the clay tablets do that makes things difficult for scholars today?"

"They broke easily. The way the book talks about our translation sounds like the scholars are making a quilt. A piece from here and a piece from there, and there are still gaps in the story."

"Good observation, Rachel. Matthew, are there any parts of the story in which you are confident that you got the whole thing?"

"Yes, the part about the kurgarra and the galatur seemed very complete."

"What made you think so?"

"Well, it started with their creation, and they did everything they were told to do in a repeated formula, so I knew I was getting it all. They were successful, so it felt like an ending."

"What do we know about the kurgarra and the galatur?"

"They don't have a sex."

"Why do you suppose that is such an important detail?"

"I don't know, but Enki sounds just like my counseling professor. He's always telling us to treat people as individuals and not as part of any class of people, to make sure the person knows they've been heard, to empathize, and never to be judgmental. I'm sure my counseling professor would say that the kurgarra and the galatur were good active listeners."

"I wonder what their sexual ambiguity has to do with treating people as individuals?"

"Well, if they don't have a sex, they might be less likely to treat people according to sexual stereotypes."

Nodding her head, Dr. Shaw said, "Perhaps. Can anybody think of any other mythological characters whose sexual ambiguity helped them communicate?"

Ted Mullins interjected, "The Greek messenger-god Hermes wasn't really sexually clear, and his son, Hermaphroditus, was both sexes. He was like the kurgarra and the galatur crossing from the realm of the living to the realm of the dead either because they are sexless or androgynous. Maybe it's important to try to look at things first from a just plain human perspective, not first as a man or woman, if one wants to be a good communicator. Maybe we're supposed to think about what the message actually means before we reference ourselves? Maybe we should understand before we judge."

"Good point, Ted, but perhaps easier said than done. What word do we use to refer to the science of interpreting literature that comes from that Greek idea?"

A few seconds of silence pass as the mental cabinets are searched. Then Ted's eyes light up. "Oh yeah! Hermeneutics."

In a smiling pause Dr. Shaw ponders the unanswerable question "Why doesn't everybody in the world want to be a teacher?" Then she says, "Let's return to our main character. In the pagan polytheism of Ancient Sumeria, how important was Inanna?"

Servat speaks up. "Inanna was the most important deity of all. Because of her, because she was a goddess rather than a god, regular Sumerian women had some status. They were involved in temple business; they owned property; they negotiated for themselves."

"Good, Servat. There does seem to be a connection. The patriarchal institutions of the second millennium BCE, with gods like Marduk or Enlil, almost eliminated women's participation in public life. And Inanna was demoted to a mere fertility goddess. But, what about Inanna's place in her own marriage? Who is her consort?"

Drew now enters the conversation with some energy. "Dumuzi just gets bossed around by Inanna. The galla abuse him. He cries like a wimp. Inanna is a great goddess, and she's married to a lowly human shepherd. In this story she has the superior status." The speech contained a palpable undercurrent of contempt for the dominated Dumuzi.

"Right, I wouldn't like to be in Dumuzi's place," responded the professor. "I have just been wondering if any of you heard about Inanna before this reading assignment?"

Crystal joins in with, "When I was visiting my sister in Raleigh, she took me to a pretty radical feminist meeting, and we sang a hymn to Inanna. I didn't really get it then, but I think I do now."

"Thanks, Crystal, Inanna is still very important in many strains of feminism. Hymns to Inanna are popular videos on YouTube. What about other powerful goddesses in our culture?"

Travis pipes up, "People today are just past that. We are more rational than those primitive cultures."

"So you don't see goddesses in your daily life?"

"No way."

Chapter 3

Dr. Shaw hesitates for a moment. "I see you grabbed a cup of coffee on your way to class. That Starbuck's logo on your cup is an almost omnipresent image in our society; is it not?"

Travis agrees, "Yea, it's everywhere."

"Could you describe it for us?"

"Well, I guess so. I'm not sure I know what it actually is."

"Is it feminine or masculine?" asks the teacher.

"Definitely feminine. It has long hair."

"Does anything in the image imply she is a sovereign?"

"For sure, she's wearing a crown."

"Is there any image above her crown to suggest what she might be ruler of?"

"I see a star; maybe she's ruler of the heavens?"

"Is there anything in the image that implies she's mythical?"

"Wow, I never noticed that she has fins. Why, she's a mermaid with two tails."

"Yes, she's sometimes called a siren, a kind of goddess in myths, and the fact that she has two tails makes her particularly powerful."

Chapter 4

All flesh is not the same flesh, but there is one kind of flesh of men, another flesh of animals, another of fish, and another of birds.

—1 Corinthians 15:39

Dr. Shaw asks the class what the first reading strategy listed on the syllabus is, and receives thirty-five blank stares. Then Servat, the only student who bothered to print out the syllabus, begins searching through her notebook. She momentarily answers, "We are supposed to note the reading assignment's genre."

"Right, and what is genre?"

Travis, with a vague feeling of wanting to give a correct answer after that last exchange, felt himself on firm ground with this. "Genre is the kind of literature that a text is, like whether it's a poem or a novel."

"Exactly," replies Dr. Shaw. "Why is it important to know the genre?"

Again, silence.

Dr. Shaw asks another question. "If I begin a story with 'once upon a time,' what genre is it?"

Crystal answers, "A fairy tale." And the whole class agrees.

"And what does that tell us about how to interpret the story?"

Matthew says. "We know it's just a made-up story."

"Right, if the author is purposefully vague about the time of the setting, a perceptive reader knows that the events never really happened at all. Does that mean that the fairy tale isn't true?"

Rachel, a bit surprised at such an easy question, responds with a quick, "Of course not, it's just fiction."

The teacher stops to consider a change in the conversational course, then she says, "On the first day of class, I asked you all to list five books you've read since the eighth grade that you enjoyed. From those lists I know that most of you have read a Harry Potter book, either *The Hobbit* or *The*

Lord of the Rings, and more than one of Lewis' Chronicles of Narnia—all fiction. So, did you see anything true about real English boarding school experiences from reading about Hogwarts? Did you recognize anything true in Bilbo Baggins's tension between the comfortable and the adventurous? Did you notice anything true about Jesus of Nazareth from reading about Aslan? . . . I suggest that often works of fiction are unconcerned about the truth of their facts, but that they are very concerned about the truth of ideas."

Travis announced, "I don't believe there is such a thing as the truth of ideas; the only kind of truth is truth about verifiable, empirical facts."

"I am sure, Travis, that the many people in our culture agree with you about that, or that, at least, they unthinkingly presuppose it in their daily decisions. But such a generalization is not true of the ancient cultures we will read in this class. And I am asking you to please read and interpret the literature according to its literary and cultural context, as best you can, before you make judgments upon it. I am not asking you to agree with anything, but only to withhold your opinion of the text until you have been careful about the question, 'What did it mean to them?'"

Travis's "I'll try" had a ring of sincerity.

"Thank you. That is all I ask . . . Now returning to our question of genre, I maintain that knowing the genre of a text arms us with help for our interpretation. My friend in California, Tremper Longman, uses a story to illustrate this idea. Who has read a work in the genre murder mystery?" Many heads nod. "Who are some of the genre's authors?"

"Agatha Christie," came a girl's voice from the back of the room.

"James Patterson," said Jason.

"Sue Grafton," chimed in someone by the window.

"Excellent examples—Now if I told you the title of this text is *Murder at Marplethorp*, what genre is it?"

"A Murder Mystery," a chorus responds.

"Right, this is how the story begins:

> The clock on the mantelpiece said ten-thirty, but someone had suggested recently that the clock was wrong. As the figure of the dead woman lay on the bed in the front room, a no less silent figure glided rapidly from the house. The only sounds to be heard were the ticking of the clock and the loud wailing of an infant.[1]

---

1. Longman, *How to Read the Psalms*, from Heather Dubrow, *Genre*.

"So, let's interpret this opening passage as though, by genre, it's a murder mystery. Who is the dead woman and how did she die?"

Amy says, "She is the murder victim; somebody killed her." The entire class agrees.

The teacher's next question is, "Who is the silent figure gliding from the house?"

Andrew offers, "That is the murderer making his escape. The whole point of the book is to figure out who he is." Again, universal agreement.

"Next interpretive question—Why is the infant crying?"

Crystal ventures, "The woman was a mother. Her baby was awakened by the violent murder, and, since the mother is dead, she isn't taking care of her child." Everybody thinks the same.

"Why is the clock important?"

Travis offers, "The clock is telling us when the woman died. The first fact a detective will want to establish is time of death. For example, every suspect's alibi depends on it." Nobody disagrees.

"You are all excellent interpreters of murder mysteries. Have any of you ever read a biography?" Most heads nod. "What does a reader expect from a generic biography?"

Matthew answers, "It's going to tell the true story of some famous person's life. The reader tries to see how the person's life experiences influenced him or her."

"Exactly. I am now going to read the opening of a biography entitled *The Personal History of David Marplethorp*:

> The clock on the mantelpiece said ten-thirty, but someone had suggested recently that the clock was wrong. As the figure of the dead woman lay on the bed in the front room, a no less silent figure glided rapidly from the house. The only sounds to be heard were the ticking of the clock and the loud wailing of an infant."

Many smiles reveal that many students are seeing how this line of questioning will go. Dr. Shaw asks the same questions of the same text. "Who is the dead woman and how did she die?"

Rachel, who had read many biographies, answers, "She is the mother of David Marplethorp, and she died in childbirth. Biographies usually begin with a birth."

"Who is the silent figure gliding from the house?"

Jason thinks it is the grief-stricken midwife, who has failed in her attempt to save the mother. Nodding heads confirm his interpretation.

Chapter 4

"Why is the infant crying?"

Rachel again—"The baby is David Marplethorp, and he's crying for his mother. Losing a mother at birth is an extraordinarily important fact about a childhood. That grief won't go away; nor will it be easy to identify. It will have a huge influence on his life."

"That it will. Why is the clock important?"

Rachel, the future nurse, again—"It establishes time of birth."

"I hope this little exercise will remind you all to pay attention to genre. Now, what genre is *The Descent of Inanna*?"

Matthew says it's a myth.

"Correct, Matthew, how did you know?"

"Well, I can see the use of all the mythic conventions listed on our handout from last week. For example, at first I thought it was very unusual and disgusting that the kurgarra and the galatur were made out of the dirt from under the fingernails of Enki. But when I was studying 'Substance of Creation' on the handout, I tried to think of why the god would have made them from that. I've heard a few people say, 'He doesn't like to get his hands dirty.' I thought perhaps it means the Enki created them to do his hard labor. When I read *Atrahsis*, I thought I was correct. In that myth it was why the gods created man."

"Very perceptive, Matthew. Can anyone think of another myth in which we obviously learn about a creature's purpose or characteristics from the substance of his or her creation?"

Ted reminds the class that the goddess Athena in Greek mythology was created from the brain of Zeus. Therefore, we should assume that she is very smart . . .

Dr. Shaw closes by reminding the class that the reading quiz on Wednesday will be on the *Enuma Elish*, and that they should refer to the list of mythic conventions as they read.

At 10:50, the bees rise and begin the hourly swarm.

Chapter 5

And Adam was not deceived, but the woman was deceived …

—1 Timothy 2:14

Holly Billingham rises from a desk in Rankin Hall at 10:50. She reels from the cognitive overload produced by her Monday anatomy lecture. Holly makes a beeline across the Avery Mall for the student union where she has staked out the perfect study venue, a little paradise in the midst of her busy days. It's only the second week of her first semester in college, and she already feels in danger of falling behind. Mondays, Wednesdays, and Fridays she has an hour break between her anatomy lecture and her freshman composition class in Avery Hall. Between those two locations is the solarium, the idyllic place to organize and begin memorizing the complexities of the human body. Above the huge plants and flowing fountains stretches a narrow loft lined with comfortable rocking chairs. The peaceful setting seems to help her get an intellectual grip. She also wonders if Kevin Parsons will be there again.

Last Monday, the very first day of classes, she had been in the rocking chair that she now considered her own. Her anatomy book had been open. He had walked past her and seemed to observe what she was doing. Her first thought of him had been that he was "checking her out," but she had long forgotten that initial impression. Wednesday, after her second lecture, he had shown up again. He took the rocking chair next to her, introduced himself, and showed her that he had the same anatomy text. He told her that he needed to prepare for Prof. Collins' twelve o'clock anatomy lecture.

"Really?" she said, "I have Collins at ten."

He looked surprised and a bit nervous. "That class is a bit frightening for me. I need it for my major, but I've never had to memorize so much."

Holly's sympathetic response was, "I know what you mean. I'm already feeling swamped. My usual confidence is melting."

Chapter 5

He asked for a summary of the ten o'clock lecture which he assumed would be repeated at noon. The process of telling him back the lecture that she had just heard was precisely what she needed to do. As she summarized for him, she created order of the material in her own mind. In high school she had always avoided group study sessions. She considered them nothing but a waste of time. But this was different; perhaps this kind of study could be really helpful for both of them. He seemed eager to have a head start on the material, and he listened attentively as she tried to explain it. Kevin had shown up again in the solarium loft on Friday. Another quality study session had resulted. Holly also needed this course for her major, nursing, and she was already beginning to depend upon their meeting to review the lecture.

She had just passed her first weekend of college. On Saturday she, Jill, and Megan had hiked the Poplar Fork Trail, watched part of the football game from their dorm window, and in the evening gone off campus to Sweet Frog for customized yogurt sundaes.

Megan had gone to an early mass on Sunday morning, but the subject of church attendance had been avoided by the two Protestants. Holly and Jill had slept in, and all three had spent most of Sunday studying. Late in the afternoon, they went next door to the McGinn Recreation Center and worked out. Now it was Monday again, and Holly was hoping Kevin would appear, along with his helpful questions. As she opened the loft door, she saw him already waiting for her.

She sat down next to him and was soon caught up in an explanation of the bones, tendons and ligaments of the foot and ankle. She exhausted her notes and knowledge well before time to leave for freshman comp, and he started a new subject.

"I live in a fraternity house over on Orchard Street, just the first right off Grand Boulevard. My frat brothers and I are having a little party on Friday evening. Would you like to come? It may be a bit boring," he admitted, "and totally drug and alcohol free, not even a DJ."

The word "fraternity" raised red flags like poppies in spring. She had been warned about frat parties by her older brother, Darren, who was at Chapel Hill. He was definitely overprotective and had unilaterally demanded that she "never go to frat parties." Her father had heard Darren's imperative and seconded it. At orientation she had heard many rules pertaining to "Greek social events," but she didn't remember them now. Kevin was a clean-cut sort, and not at all bad looking. He was obviously a serious student, and had specifically stated no drugs or alcohol. Last week he mentioned that he attended the Baptist Church adjoining campus on College Street. But those mental red flags fluttered still. So Holly responded noncommittally. "If I did come, I'd want to bring my friends, Jill and Megan."

Kevin liked the idea. "My frat brothers won't mind; bring them along. I'd like to meet your friends."

Holly Billingham, Jill Kelly, and Megan Clery were old friends. They grew up together in an upper-middle-class neighborhood, Asheford Green, in Concord, a suburb of Charlotte, North Carolina. They had often gone to different schools, and did not share many of the same special interests. They had, nevertheless, been friends as long as they could remember. During the school year they had often gone weeks without seeing one another. But they had always spent a lot of time together during summers. Their parents were friends, and Holly's brother, Darren, dated Jill's sister, Katie.

During their senior year of high school, they were delighted to discover that the others were also applying to Blue Ridge State. Holly wanted to be accepted as a nursing major, Jill was hoping for interior design, and Megan sought a place in the Reich College of Education. They decided that they would try to room together if they were all accepted, but they worried that two of them would get in and not the third. Amazingly, they had all been accepted, and now they were suitemates, along with a girl from Asheville, Lauren Davis, in Gorman Hall. They had loved their dormitory right away. They were on ninth floor and just across the street from Kidd Brewer Stadium—right in the middle of football hoopla. Their parents liked that they would be together, for there existed mutual respect among these families. The three girls had survived high school together relatively unscathed. The parents thought they would be good for one another.

About six thirty Monday evening Holly brought the troubling subject up. The three were eating in Privette Hall, the dining commons near their dormitory. Before placing the forkful of mashed potatoes in her mouth, Holly said, "Do you remember me telling you about the guy I've been studying anatomy with in the solarium? Well, today he asked us to a fraternity party on Friday evening."

In the silence, Holly recognized the two other fields of red flags springing up. Jill eventually said, "I'm pretty sure my Dad would blow a gasket if he knew I went to a frat party."

Holly reassured her with, "Kevin said that there wouldn't be any alcohol or drugs, and it would be just a small, quiet event" (borrowing the PC term from orientation and carefully avoiding "party").

Chapter 5

Megan, likewise leery, asked, "Where is the frat house?"

Holly replied, "It's just behind King Street. I know a little trail between Hubbub and Poplar Bagelry. We could quickly walk over. If we cross the Raley parking lot, walk the half block up Blue Ridge Street, and up the little shortcut, we'd be in the house's backyard in five minutes."

Jill asked, "What's Kevin like?"

Holly looked more confident than she felt. "He's cute and clean-cut. He seems like a nice guy. He takes anatomy seriously."

Then Megan offered the persuasive facts when she said, "My dad was in Kappa Gamma Pi, and he's still good friends with those guys. To hear them talk, they must have been pretty nerdy. They're all serious Catholics, and I know the fraternity volunteered together at a soup kitchen in a church basement. They were at East Carolina, but they were not rowdy."

Megan's father was now the principal of the large Catholic high school in Charlotte, where her stepmother was a reading specialist. None of the girls could imagine Dr. Clery as anything but law abiding and responsible. If Meg's dad was a frat boy, they couldn't all be bad.

In spite of a unanimous sense of reluctance, they agreed to go. But they pledged to each other that if any one of them wanted to leave, they would all go with no questions asked. It was also agreed that no one was to speak of the "event" with anybody from Concord.

Chapter 6

But you shall do nothing to the young woman; there is in the young woman no sin deserving of death, for just as when a man rises against his neighbor and kills him, even so is this matter . . . The young woman cried out, but there was no one to save her.

—Deuteronomy 22:26–27

All four girls from Gorman 924 had sushi together in Privette on Friday around six o'clock. They invited Lauren, their roommate from Asheville, to go the frat party with them. But she was a flutist and had her first college performance that evening. Reaching River Street after dinner, Holly, Jill, and Megan crossed, heading for the Raley parking lot. Lauren went left toward the Troyhill Music Center.

In less than five minutes the three were off campus, through the restaurant parking lot, up the fifty feet of trail through some dense trees, and knocking on the front door of a large brick house on Orchard Street. The frat house had a well-used look, but was in decent repair and very tidy. Kevin Parsons answered the door, and when the girls were shown in, all red flags were lowered. Some good bluegrass was playing at a modest decibel. They could see into the living room where a group of seven student-types, with their backs to the newcomers and facing a large TV, were playing *Scene It*? Kevin said, "I'll introduce you in a few minutes when they finish this game. Would you like some punch?" He was already drinking some.

A large cut-glass punch bowl and matching cups were on the dining table, along with a bowl of hummus and a basket of pita chips. Megan recognized the punch bowl as one just like her grandmother's, surprisingly old fashioned for a bunch of young guys—but certainly cheap in a thrift store. Jill was impressed by the presentation, she couldn't imagine her brother, Trevor, making things look this nice. Lemon slices were floating in the bowl of carbonated punch, probably some soda and orange juice, thought Holly.

Chapter 6

Kevin served Holly first, and she took a sip. Jill and Megan watched for any sign from Holly of its being spiked. They all planned on drinking modestly after they were 21, but they didn't want to get in trouble for underage drinking now. Holly simply smiled reassuringly, and they all had some. As Holly was taking her second sip, she had a fleeting remembrance of a warning given at orientation. Kevin began passing around some high quality darts, and invited them to throw at the big, pub-style board on the dining room wall. After a few minutes of this activity, Jill felt like sitting on the old sofa that was also in the dining room. Holly and Megan joined her . . .

Chapter 7

And the sons of Jacob came out of the field when they heard it: and the men were grieved, and they were very wroth, because he had wrought folly in Israel in lying with Jacob's daughter: which thing ought not to be done.

—Genesis 34:7

Following a vague interval that they somehow knew was longer than it felt, Megan said to the others, who were still sitting on the sofa with her, "I'm really sorry to be a party-pooper, but I feel like I might be getting the flu. I'm sort of nauseous."

"No problem, Meg, we'll all go," replied Jill as she rose to exit. But she almost sat down again with a feeling of having just stepped off a merry-go-round. Holly quickly agreed that it was time to leave, for she wasn't feeling that great herself. Kevin politely asked if he should walk them back to their dorm. But they all refused the offer because it was such a short way. They thanked him and apologized for needing to leave his party early. He saw them to the door, and as they were leaving, said to Holly, "See you on Monday in the solarium." He made his salutation with an insinuating smile that she did not like. She imagined him as a snake in her little study paradise.

After he closed the door, they made their way around the house, down the little trail, between the restaurant and bagelry, and down the half block of Blue Ridge Street. As they walked again across the Raley lot, Megan suggested that maybe the punch had been spiked a bit, "For I feel sort of drunk." Holly didn't say so, but she felt like she had after she had made love with Aaron during her senior year. As soon as they reached the suite, each of them used the bathroom and went immediately to bed . . .

Lauren only played in the first half of the concert and so left the Troyhill at intermission. She returned to Gorman before nine, expecting to arrive there long before the others. To her surprise, they were not only home, but all were sound asleep on top of their bedspreads. And nobody

Chapter 7

had bothered to put on her pajamas. It made her curious to hear about that frat party. Seeing the unusual opportunity to catch up on some sleep, Lauren was in bed by ten o'clock.

Gorman 924 was like all suites on the ninth floor. Two bedrooms just big enough for bunk beds, two closets and two built-in desks, joined by a small, common sitting room with a large window. 924, 926, and 928 overlooked the football stadium. The bathroom, furnished with a toilet, shower, and long counter with two sinks opened from between the bedrooms into both. Jill and Lauren shared one bedroom and Holly and Megan the other.

Holly and Megan were early risers, but Jill was usually even earlier. When Lauren woke at nine, she lay in her top bunk and listened for their conversation to filter in from the common room. She heard nothing at all. She thought that perhaps they went for an early workout at the McGinn? Maybe they decided to go to Baguette Boy Kitchen for bagel sandwiches? They probably didn't want to wake her to ask if she wanted to come along. Did they leave her a note? Descending the bunk ladder, Lauren was very surprised to see Jill still asleep. She was exactly as she had seen her the night before. Jill had not ever put on her pajamas or gotten under her blankets. Lauren was becoming alarmed. She went into the other bedroom to discover that Holly and Meg were also exactly as they had been. She just knew something was desperately wrong with this scene. Lauren advanced to Holly's bottom bunk and began shaking her. Holly groggily opened her eyes, mumbled "g'morning," and promptly fell back to sleep. Lauren returned to her own room and fiercely jostled Jill into consciousness. That state was short-lived. With a slurred "not feelin' well," Jill returned to oblivion. Then Lauren spied something that sent her into panic. Peeking out above the top of the same jeans Jill had worn at dinner last night and below the ribbing of the same sweater, she saw Megan's paisley underwear stained with blood.

Lauren immediately reached for her phone and called the number her mother had entered onto her opening screen.

"Campus Police Emergency Desk."

"I want to report three possible sexual assaults. We're in Gorman Hall suite 924..."

Chapter 8

May the Lord answer you in the day of trouble;
May the name of the God of Jacob defend you;
May He send you help from the sanctuary,
And strengthen you out of Zion.

—Psalm 20:1–2

A CAMPUS POLICEMAN AND an open-faced woman from the counseling center arrived not ten minutes later. Jill, Holly, and Megan weren't aware of their entrance. Lauren gave a clear, brief explanation of the reason for her call. The counselor turned her attention to the other three and was able, with the policeman's help, to bring them to the surface.

The woman, Janet, was calm, kind, and efficient. In answer to her question, "Have you been sexually assaulted?" Jill raised her shoulders and asked, rather than stated, "I don't know?" Holly said, "Maybe." Megan said, "No." When Janet asked Jill why she was wearing Megan's underwear, Jill looked down, lifted her sweater and definitely stated, "I don't know." With Lauren's help as to times, Janet was gently able to get the basic story of the night before out of the other three. She was particularly interested in the details of the punch, and how they each felt on the way home. She several times reminded all four of them that they had done nothing wrong. Megan vaguely wondered why she said that, of course they hadn't.

After she understood what she could for the time being, Janet quietly told the girls that she suspected that they had been drugged. "I am concerned that you may have hidden injuries. I would like you to come with me down to the Watauga Medical Center and have a forensic exam by a sexual assault nurse before you have a shower, use the toilet, or change your clothes. The exam will be paid for, but it will probably take several hours. It is your choice."

Jill's "Well, OK" was confirmed by the other two.

Chapter 8

A minute later Lauren was all alone in 924 holding in her hand a copy of "How to Help Victims of Sexual Assault," and holding in her mind Janet's unqualified statement that she had been a good friend and had acted wisely. She was also left with the promise that another counselor from the center would be stopping by soon to check on her.

Down at the hospital Jill, Holly, and Megan all learned that they had sex within the past twenty-four hours with at least two men. But no evidence of drugs showed in their urines. Janet explained that this lack of evidence confirmed her suspicion that GHB, a drug known locally as Georgia Home Boy, had been in the punch. Unfortunately, this lack of evidence could not be used by the prosecutor. The SANE kits were stored, and several decisions made. Yes, they wanted protection for STD's. Yes, they would take an emergency contraceptive pill called ella. Yes, they would report the "event" to the Poplar Police since it happened off campus. Yes, Megan would return tomorrow for some minor gynecological out-patient surgery. Yes, they wanted to prosecute Kevin Parsons. Yes, they would talk to a deputy DA for Watauga County. Yes, they felt safe returning to Gorman 924. Yes, they felt "yes" was the right thing to do. But yes, it was the most horrible day of their lives. Yes, they felt an overwhelming and crushing vulnerability. Yes, they were exhausted in every way possible. Yes, they felt ashamed, guilty, betrayed, and violated. Yes, they felt stupid and naïve. Yes, they were victimized and powerless, in spite of many kind people helping them.

As they were preparing to go, Holly said, "I now know what it means that women are the weaker vessels. Paul's letter just doesn't go far enough. Women are objectified and treated as inanimate meat, non-persons so vulnerable they have no power over their own bodies. We are seen as things to use." They all cried into a group hug.

None of the girls heard the sexual assault nurse say to Janet, just as they were leaving, "Because of her dates, regularity, and exam, I think it very likely that Jill ovulated only yesterday."

"Well, let's hope nothing comes of it," replied Janet quietly.

Jill, Holly, and Megan experienced a revolutionary reassessment of the world that Saturday. That the counselors, lawyers, doctors, law enforcement personnel, nurses, etc. could carry on business as usual, that this kind of trauma was expected by them and delivered every working day, that their utter disaster was simply routine for these helping professionals—showed these three very young women that the world was a much more deeply sinister place than they had realized. And being a woman took on a new and unwanted meaning, a meaning they had been trying their whole lives to deny.

Chapter 9

For my days are consumed like smoke,
And my bones are burned like a hearth.
My heart is stricken and withered like grass,
So that I forget to eat my bread.
Because of the sound of my groaning
My bones cling to my skin.
I am like a pelican of the wilderness;
I am like an owl of the desert.
I lie awake,
And am like a sparrow alone on the housetop.

—Psalm 102:3–7

Sunday morning Megan didn't wake, because she had never really gone to sleep. But she became more self-aware by hearing herself emit a sound about half-way between a groan and a cry. She heard Holly sit up in her bottom bunk. The groan-cry formed itself into, "Oh Holly, I wish I didn't have to go down to that darn hospital again this morning. But I know I should; the tear is still bleeding a bit."

Holly asked, "Janet said she'd stay with you; do you want me to come along?" She immediately wished she hadn't said it. If Megan asked her to come, what would she do? She couldn't bear to go to the place of humiliation again.

"I doubt if you want to go down there any more than I do," said Megan.

"I didn't say I want to go, but I do want you to be supported," replied Holly.

"It's OK," came out with a deep exhale, "I'll just go with Janet. But please pray for me. I really don't have the strength for this."

Chapter 9

Just then they heard the door close and Lauren call out, "Breakfast time." She set a brown paper Baguette Boy bag on the coffee table and pulled out four of their favorite bagel sandwiches, "Green Eggs and Ham." The eggs were only green because pesto sauce was spread on the bagel, normally a tantalizing meal. But nothing would be normal anymore. And none of the three victims felt like eating.

They all wondered how Lauren knew they would not leave Gorman 924, even to go across the street to Privette for breakfast. "Thanks, Lauren," came in a genuinely thankful but unenthusiastic chorus.

Holly immediately sat down, unwrapped the treat, and bit into the breakfast sandwich. It really was delicious. It brought a small, if shallow, sense of comfort. It was nutritious; and more importantly, it was she who decided that it would penetrate her body. Megan couldn't take a single bite, so Holly ate hers as well as her own. Like Megan, Jill refused anything penetrating her from the outside. All three women were desperate to exert control over their bodies, healthy or not.

The day progressed with tears and regretful talk until Megan returned with Janet from the hospital. Janet stayed for some therapeutic conversation for a while, but it was the three victims that had long trusted one another who helped themselves on the road to healing. They knew each other well and had been open with one another for years. They had endured a common calamity, and they were able to honestly voice intense emotions.

They did not feel the same, but there were common threads which bound them together like cables. They suffered, but they were not suffering alone as so many others had to do. They had each other, and they all three had a vital relationship with a God who they did not believe would abandon them now. All three had been taught from childhood that one could not expect to escape misery in a fallen world or to always understand why God allowed tragedies. They all depended on Providence and accepted that suffering could be redemptive and sanctifying.

At about three o'clock in the afternoon, Megan said, "I've never been attracted to alcohol as a stress relief; but right now; if there was a bottle of whiskey (which I detest) on the table, I'd drink it, hoping to offload this crushing feeling of shame. That is not how I want to get through this. I need you two to tell me if I'm self-destructive. I don't think I'll be able to see it—I'm in a fog."

Holly added, "I'm more likely to try and eat my way through this. I gained fifteen pounds when I broke up with Aaron, and that shame was nothing to this."

Jill said, "I could easily become anorexic. All I want to do right now is go for a run. If I could really hammer for three hours or so, I think I might sleep tonight."

But they prayed together instead. Megan didn't drink, and Holly only ate the third sandwich leftover from breakfast. Jill went for a run, but promised to do only three miles. Megan and Jill still had not eaten, but they agreed to go to Privette in the morning as usual and eat something.

With a rehearsal in the Rosen and research for her theory class in the Troyhill Music Library, Lauren didn't return to the suite until six thirty Monday evening. She was then updated on some resolutions made by the other three.

There had been no classes on Monday because it was Labor Day. They were all deeply relieved. None of them felt like going to class. But they all decided it would be good for them to go, regardless of whether they could concentrate. They decided that they would fight together for the new normal, whatever that was. They resolved to make one another accountable to attend all their classes. Although Lauren was not tempted to ditch, she would perhaps be in the suite if they had. She promised to challenge them if they were in the suite when they shouldn't be.

None of them had classes between five and six o'clock p.m., and they decided to swim each weekday afternoon. Even when they had gone to different schools, the three had swum together in the summers on the McInnis team in Concord. It was the one sport they all enjoyed. They knew they should take special care of themselves now and committed to making one another accountable for a swim workout each day. Lauren was seldom available at that time, so she wouldn't join them. But she agreed to support that resolution.

She also agreed to a new resolution they made to not keep junk food in the common room. Eating between meals in front of Holly would be a temptation to her.

They had already established a quiet time in the suite between six thirty and seven a.m., but it now took on the importance of survival. Megan read through a lectionary, Holly had a Bible reading schedule, and Jill used a devotional guide her mother had given her. Lauren didn't go in for spiritual disciplines; indeed, she had no religious practice or faith. But she

Chapter 9

was glad the others followed this routine because it gave her sole use of the bathroom every morning at that time.

Lauren pressed them for one more resolution she thought would be good for them. "You need to tell your parents."

Jill explained. "We've talked about that. You're right; we need to do it. But we're not ready. You can make us accountable for that—but not yet."

Megan explained, "I'm eager to tell my mom; but if I do, she'll tell my dad and probably Holly and Jill's moms. They need to tell their own families, and the news will be devastating to all of them. It is just more than we can cope with right now. Tomorrow we're all going to call our moms when we know they won't pick up and leave a message that we'll call on the weekend. Hopefully we'll tell them then. We all talked to them on Friday, so they won't be worried. We are sooo dreading it."

Tuesday evening as all four residents of Gorman 924 were busy at their desks, Holly's phone rang.

"Hello, Ms. Billingham, this is Detective Steve Konnenberg from the Poplar Police. I met you Saturday morning at Watauga hospital. Is this a good time to call?'

"As good as any," replied Holly without enthusiasm.

"May two detectives and I come over in an hour or so? One would meet with Megan on the McGinn patio, and one with Jill in a Privette booth. I would bring Janet, and we could talk with you and Lauren in the dorm room."

"One moment, please."

Holly laid her cell phone face-down on her desk and went into the common area where Jill and Megan were attempting to study. Lauren came in from the other bedroom.

"The detective we met on Saturday from the Poplar Police wants to come over this evening with Janet and two others and talk to us individually." The emotional pressure in the room invisibly, but palpably escalated, seeking some vent. Jill provided it after a deep pause.

"Let's just get it over with! We'll need to talk with them again sometime."

Megan replied, "I could not endure tomorrow if I knew we were doing it tomorrow night—the sooner the better."

Holly returned to her desk, and the others heard through the bedroom door. "OK, we're all home."

An hour later Holly faced Detective Konnenberg, who was sitting in the other common room chair. The detective forged ahead. "I'm sorry, ma'am, to report that no Kevin Parsons has been registered at Blue Ridge in the last twenty-five years. Nobody at the Baptist Church on College Street has ever met a Kevin Parsons or could remember anybody answering his description. Professor Collins does not have a twelve o'clock anatomy class.

"There are eight men now living at the Beta Alpha Delta fraternity house on Orchard Street. But that chapter of the Beta Alpha Delta has had its charter revoked by the university. A department located in the Clemmons Student Union called CSIL or Center for Student Involvement & Leadership monitors Greek life on campus. The director tells me that her office has had many complaints about Beta Alpha Delta. Spring semester a girl at one of their parties photographed with her phone several proofs of noncompliance with CSIL rules, among them an open punch bowl. This means that the fraternity is not recognized by the university and can do nothing on campus, but that it is still a member of the national fraternity. This entitles the Blue Ridge chapter to excellent legal counsel and insurance. Any action we take against these frat boys will be hotly contested by the best. We will need strong evidence to prosecute.

"On the evening of August 30 seven of them had gone skating at a rink at the corner of the 321 and the 421 in Vilas, only ten minutes away. The eighth member of the fraternity, Tom Shelton, is a part-time employee of the skating rink. He told me that he sold his frat brother, Drew Mitchell, seven drinks at the snack bar there that evening. Earlier in the week Andrew had lost a bet on a dart game at the house, so the drinks at the rink were his payment of that debt. Andrew claims that his frat brothers, Marty Wallace, Allen Halter, and Grif Thompson rode with him in his champagne-colored 2010 Mercedes sedan to the rink. The other three, Robbie Green, Cliff Miller, and Salvatori Cinelli, went to the rink in Sal's old, blue Mini Cooper. The boys say nobody was in the locked frat house when they left about five thirty to go skating, and nobody was home when they returned. The neighbor across the street confirmed that those two cars returned noisily together about ten o'clock that night and that the house was unusually quiet for a weekend until they returned. The neighbor did not see any cars in the driveway earlier in the evening. All eight residents are registered students at Blue Ridge State, and all eight deny being home between five thirty and ten o'clock Friday."

The detective asked several more questions in a very routine tone. And then a few Holly could tell were of special interest to him.

Chapter 9

"Did this 'Kevin Parsons' give you directions on how to get to the party?"

"Yes, he said to go up Grand and take the first right," Holly answered.

"But you and your friends did not go that way?"

"No, during orientation weekend I met a girl who lives in an apartment on Orchard Street. Our group was getting a tour of King Street, and she wanted to get a sweatshirt from her apartment because she was getting a bit chilly. I followed her because I wanted to see inside an off-campus apartment. She led me up and down a little short-cut through the trees."

"Do you remember seeing any particular cars in the parking lot as you walked between the restaurants?"

"Well, not specifically. But I do remember that Hubbub seemed very crowded. And that Poplar Bagelry was closed, yet there were some cars behind the bagelry."

"Do you remember any specifics about any of those cars?"

Holly stopped and tried to relive that phase of the catastrophic pilgrimage.

"I think the car that we walked next to, on our left, was a dark-colored van, the kind of van that has solid panels instead of windows. It had backed in, and was facing the driveway."

Detective Konnenberg thanked her and ended with, "I'm sorry, but my investigation is, so far, inconclusive and has produced no arrests. I will update you when there is anything significant to report if that is what you and your friends want."

"Yes, I think so, but I'll talk about it with Jill and Megan. I know I want these guys prevented from hurting other girls. And I would love to be darn sure that I'm not sitting with them in class or being assigned a group project to work on with one of them. I think the others will feel the same way. Do you think they really went skating? Do you think these frat boys did this to us?" implored Holly.

Detective Konnenberg's measured response spoke sympathy and a genuine desire for justice. "I cannot say; I don't yet have evidence for any conclusion. But I will tell you that I have had several investigations dead end at that frat house. When I came to this post five years ago, it was on the department's radar then. And I can tell you that my daughter will not go to a party at that house for all the tea in China." Holly felt that the detective both respected and believed her. She had been pulled over once by a police officer for rolling through a stop sign. Even though he had just given her a warning, he used the opportunity to make her feel dumb. She was thankful that this guy wasn't that sort.

After the police left, the three compared interviews. The series of questions Holly had perceived as routine had been asked of the other three. The others had given similar answers, and the girls thought his would confirm the truthfulness of their story.

Holly asked, "Did your detectives ask you about the cars in the parking lot by Hubbub?"

Jill answered, "Yes, I said there was a black van at the bottom of the trail."

Megan added, "I told him that we passed a GMC panel van, but I didn't remember the color. I knew it was one because my uncle has one. He would always take our bikes to the family picnics in it."

Holly responded, "Wow, we all remembered such an apparently insignificant detail. My memory was so hazy, but we all noticed it—so it must have been there."

Chapter 10

...Entreat me not to leave you,
Or to turn back from following after you;
For wherever you go, I will go.

—Ruth 1:16

Nora began the descent through the small but dense forest. Yesterday Poplar had received an unseasonably early snow. It was only the 21st of October. Only last week the trees had been ablaze with autumn foliage. She especially loved the golds. But today the grey poles of denuded poplars rose through the lower layer of snow-covered rhododendron. As the cold breeze struck her face, she huddled inside her jacket and wondered for the millionth time why she was here. The dwarves' dirge-like song kept replaying in her mind.

> Far over the misty mountains cold
>
> To dungeons deep and caverns old
>
> We must away, ere break of day,
>
> To find our long-forgotten gold.[1]

It had all happened so quickly. Luke had seen, by the merest chance, the job announcement on the Saints' Resources website. The skills-required list, amazingly disparate, fitted him like a glove: critical incident stress debriefing and heavy equipment operation, Christian counseling and a Class A driver's license, paramedic training and diesel mechanics, knowledge of the building trades and woodcutting/arbor care. Luke's thirty years as fire captain/paramedic, leader of San Luis Obispo County's critical incident stress debriefing team, builder of their two homes on the Central Coast, and director of the Presbyterian Church's Stephen's Ministry program

---

1. Tolkien, *The Hobbit*, 31.

apparently uniquely qualified him in North American Disaster Relief for Saints' Resources.

Luke had retired four years ago in excellent health from the Atascadero Fire Department. At fifty-three, he immediately appreciated regularly sleeping through the night. He had returned to college planning to take a master's in counseling, probably from Gordon-Conwell Theological Seminary or some other program without a residency requirement, get an MFCC, and provide help and support for people going through troubles.

But he had been getting impatient. He had been accustomed to helping people experiencing severe trauma and going through life-shattering crises. Sitting in an office talking to people who weren't getting along with each other was losing its attraction. While he thoroughly enjoyed academic learning, he wasn't feeling really useful to others. And he was frequently distracted by going outside to "fix things."

After receiving Luke's resume, Saints' Resources had immediately requested a telephone interview. And Nora had gone online to explore universities near Poplar, North Carolina. She had been teaching rhetoric at both Cal Poly and Cuesta College for the past fifteen years and was professionally stuck. In spite of excellent teaching evaluations by peers and students and regular, quality publications, she was still not on a tenure track and was excluded from courses she wanted to teach. It wasn't that she particularly wanted tenure, but she did want to teach literature and have a full-time schedule at one place. California economics promised even more stress upon public academia; Nora's vocational frustration was likely to increase in California.

In a moment, research revealed Poplar as a beautiful small town with a large state university. Blue Ridge was part of the UNC system with an up-and-coming English department that particularly needed publishing PhDs willing to teach both British and world literature. Nora was quickly offered an attractive full-time schedule with verbal assurance that continuing excellent evaluations would bring permanent full-time status. New tenure hires were already in the works. Nora saw that more as evidence of institutional and departmental health than as a personal attraction. As permanent full-time without tenure, Nora would be playing her academic strong suits and getting benefits, without the pressure of unwanted committee involvement or "brownie-point" publishing. Luke and Nora were both offered attractive jobs in late November, moved across the country after Christmas and their regular family vacation at Lake Tahoe, and began work in January.

Chapter 10

The big change excited their strongly developed sense of adventure, but that change had a down side. Nora's parents were in Laguna Beach, where both she and Luke had grown up. And after Luke's father had died, his mother had moved to Atascadero. Their daughter Blythe, son-in-law Carl, and two-year-old granddaughter Olivia lived in San Diego. Their son Kyle, daughter-in-law Jane, five-year-old grandson, Clayton, and two-year-old granddaughter, Hunter, lived in King's Beach on the north shore of Lake Tahoe. The call of God seemed to conflict with close family ties. While divine guidance seemed apparent and the jobs compelling, the feeling was as of being torn up by the roots. Nobody in California needed daily help, and the status quo continued; but those circumstances could so easily change. Luke and Nora decided not to sell the house in Atascadero.

Nora's parents, Marilyn and Robert Bostick, had another daughter, Joy, who had recently lost her husband to cancer. She lived nearby in Corona del Mar and was an occupational therapist at Hoag. Nora knew she could trust Joy to tune into her parent's needs as only one could who lived in the area. Her brother Mark was willing to do what he could for them, but he lived in New York City where he was a journalist for NPR. Joy's daughter, Astrid, and son-in-law, Dylan, were both physicians at Hoag and attentive to their grandparents. Even with Nora on the other side of the country, at least the medical side of her parent's care was in better hands than her own.

Luke was an only child, so the care network for Sally Shaw was not as deep. Sally refused to move or fly, so bringing her to Poplar wasn't an option. This was perhaps the weakest link in the move, but at present her health was good. She lived on a street with several close, helpful neighbors, and had many other friends.

So here was Nora, a cultural fish-out-of-water, a woman used to walking barefoot in the sand now walking in sorel boots through a snowy forest to work. And it was only late October.

Nora wondered how this day would look to the young woman, whom Mae had called Jill, and whom Nora would meet tomorrow afternoon. Would she feel like she was entering an early dormancy, her pregnancy coming too early in this season of her life? Jill had perhaps dreamed of becoming pregnant in her late twenties or early thirties within the security of a loving marriage and after her university education. Now she was pregnant after just turning nineteen, a victim of rape, and only at the beginning of her degree program. Nora tearfully prayed for Jill.

Cormac Bruce had suggested in August to Nora the mentoring program at Promise Pregnancy Center. Cormac served on the board, and his church supported the ministry at Promise in various ways. She and Luke had had Ryan and Georgia Lowton over for dinner. Ryan was the executive director at Promise. He was interested in Luke's experience mentoring men through the crisis pregnancies of their girlfriends and in Nora's desire to help out at Promise. Ryan had introduced Nora to Mae Jacobs, the director of client services there. Nora had applied and been trained as a mentor for Promise.

After lecturing and holding an office hour tomorrow morning, Nora would walk over to Promise on Howard Street where Mae would introduce her to Jill Kelly, her first client.

But right now she should think through her lecture on Genesis 1 for world lit.

Chapter 11

Now the story of Christ is simply a true myth: a myth working on us the same way as the others, but with this tremendous difference that it really happened: and one must be content to accept it in the same way, remembering that it is God's myth where the others are men's myths...

—C. S. Lewis, letter to Arthur Greeves, October 18, 1931

The students had picked up a handout that was a skeleton outline of her plan for today's class. Dr. Shaw began lecturing at ten a.m. sharp by reading from Genesis 1, the text due for today:

> Then God said, "Let Us make man in Our image, according to Our likeness; let them have dominion over the fish of the sea, over the birds of the air, and over the cattle, over all the earth and over every creeping thing that creeps on the earth." So God created man in His *own* image; in the image of God He created him; male and female He created them. Then God blessed them, and God said to them, "Be fruitful and multiply; fill the earth and subdue it; have dominion over the fish of the sea, over the birds of the air, and over every living thing that moves on the earth."
>
> And God said, "See, I have given you every herb *that* yields seed which *is* on the face of all the earth, and every tree whose fruit yields seed; to you it shall be for food. Also, to every beast of the earth, to every bird of the air, and to everything that creeps on the earth, in which *there is* life, *I have given* every green herb for food"; and it was so. Then God saw everything that He had made, and indeed *it was* very good. So the evening and the morning were the sixth day.

Nora's own voice began, "We cannot overstate the importance of the foundational narrative; the rest of the Bible is built upon it. If we get the first three chapters of Genesis wrong, we will necessarily go wrong in our interpretation all the way through. All Judeo/Christian thought is built upon this narrative. Even Jesus of Nazareth confronts gender "test questions" of the Pharisees with these bedrock principles established before the fall.[1] So why did I ask you to use the same mythic conventions handout with this text?"

Ted was quick to respond with, "You want us to first read Genesis in the same way we read other books. You want us to understand the narrative as literature before we apply it in a devotional or an authoritative way. Otherwise we'll misunderstand it and apply it wrongly. You're not saying it is necessarily and merely just a human document. You aren't denying it may be revelation, but that we understand the story in the same way we understand other stories."

"You understand me very well, Ted," confirmed Dr. Shaw. "We do not get another picture of untainted marriage until Revelation 19. According to the text, all marriages between the bookends include the effects of hearts hardened by sin.[2] Realistic narratives after Genesis 3 contain both description and prescription. That King David had many wives is descriptive, not prescriptive. Polygamy was prevalent, but not condoned. Several clear principles emerge in Genesis 1:26–31 that emphasize sexual equality by God's design, all of which deconstruct subordination and dominance according to gender. What might some of those principles be?"

Rachel confidently asserted, "Men and women are both created in the image and likeness of God. I think that means that human beings come in two sexes which both, like God, are rational, moral, and creative beings. In their own limited way they share in God's infinite capacity for those things."

"Surely it does mean that, Rachel."

Crystal said, "They both communicate and relate with each other and with God."

Mathew added, "Yeah, men and women are personal; I mean they have personalities. They're self-conscious creatures with the ability to learn stuff. They can't get exhaustive knowledge like God, but like God, they can know."

Servat said, "Men and women are both called human. So they are, first, the same kind of creature and second, male or female."

"You're right Servat, but what generic convention makes you think so?" asked her teacher.

After a pause Servat replied, "The sequence of creation—as creation goes from day to day, creatures are more personal. The people are made

---

1. See Matthew 19:3–6 and Mark 10:2–9 with Genesis 1:27 and 2:24.
2. Matthew 19:8.

Chapter 11

on the last day, and that makes it seem like they are the highest form of creation. Only the people are made in the image of God, and that's what makes them special."

"Right," affirms the professor, "humans of either sex share a common status of dignity at the pinnacle of earthly creation. According to this text, both are on the same level in the hierarchy of being. Both are lower than God and angels and higher than animals. Their class is human; they share a common category. Any other observations on the paragraph beginning at verse 26 and ending with verse 28?"

Andrew said, "This God doesn't seem to be concerned with overpopulation. It's like he's just wanting them to have lots of kids." This comment sent Dr. Shaw, in her own mind, totally off topic. Out of left field the thought came to her, "I am glad that Drew does not sit near either Rachel or Dana. They are particularly vulnerable to something about him."

She immediately scolded herself. "Nora, you do not know what's going on inside your student. You are thinking ill of him without any solid evidence." She then raised a prayer for forgiveness. She nevertheless received the idea, when she noticed Ted sitting behind Dana, that she could trust Ted to understand that "Love your neighbor as yourself" was not qualified by sexual orientation. No matter how his family may vote on gay marriage, Ted would treat Dana with respect. Nora was drawn back into the stream of conversation by Travis's voice.

He agreed with Andrew in accordance with his secular culture, but entirely without Andrew's uncomfortable edge. "Yeah, and words like 'subdue' and 'have dominion' seem like the god is giving the people *carte blanche* to do whatever they want with the environment."

Dr. Shaw said, "I think Andrew is quite right that the command to 'Be fruitful and multiply' contains an unqualified endorsement for procreation, at least before the fall. However, I do not see that as degrading to or regardless of the environment. To 'have dominion' has always been interpreted by theologians to mean a responsible stewardship. 'Dominion' entails an obligation to care for and protect. To clear cut a forest, pollute a stream, or wantonly decimate an animal population violate this stewardship. The creations on days one through five declare the glory of this God and express the beauty of their creator; they, therefore, deserve respect and appreciation. How does the next paragraph, however, present an entirely different relationship to the natural world than any myths we have studied so far?"

Jason supplied the idea that "the god here gave all the plants and animals to humans for their sake, and the people were supposed to use them for food. The people are above plants and animals in a hierarchy. In the Pagan myths we've read, the people worship nature. Their gods and goddesses are personifications of nature. The people worship, rather than responsibly use, nature—In this Genesis story the god is above and outside nature."

Travis reflected, "This seems arrogant. We are animals ourselves, and we are dependent on nature. Plants and animals have just as much right to be here as we do."

Jason asked Travis, "So do you have the moral right to eat the chicken sandwich I saw you chowing down last night in Privette?"

The question produced a deep hush in the classroom. Many were thinking something like, "Of course I have a right to eat a chicken sandwich." Some thoughts contained addenda such as "so long as the vegetables are organically grown and the chicken is free range." But without some sort of hierarchy which allowed an animal or plant to be killed for the sake of some higher creature, "Did one have the right to eat a chicken sandwich, regardless of the sustainability of its production?"

Travis' honest reply was, "I don't know."

Jason commented, "Maybe you have a right to eat the sandwich because the lettuce, tomato, and chicken do not have souls. I've always thought that the main difference between people and the other creatures was that they had a soul. I don't really see that explained here. Isn't it important in this worldview to think about humans having a body and a soul?"

"Perhaps not here . . . but maybe in the next chapter?" suggested Ted.

Dr. Shaw had moved to the side of the classroom and enjoyed the students asking and answering their own questions. For their curiosity and honesty she offered a prayer of thanksgiving. The classroom ambiance that supported this quality of conversation was not easy to create; she had often failed. To get students to provide what they are convinced is the right answer requires little skill. "Teaching is like parenting," she thought, "You know you have succeeded when you have worked yourself out of a job."

Ted said, "Well at least men and women are blessed alike. No gift of herb, tree, or any food is given according to gender, but enjoyed as common provision direct from the hand of God. Reproduction is not only mutual, but interdependent; they need one another to 'be fruitful and multiply.' And as with everything else before the fall, it is 'good,' good in the full philosophical sense, related to beauty and truth, a perfection of goodness beyond our present understanding. Men and women are given joint dominion over the rest of creation. This cultural mandate calls all humans to benevolent vice-regency. The pronoun 'them' in verses 26, 27, and 28 clearly refer to Adam and Eve as plural, representing both sexes. What is emphasized in the passage, particularly in the phrase translated 'male and female' is equality of dominion. Both Adam and Eve are directly responsible to God for their stewardship of earthly creation. But neither natural man nor natural woman has dominion over Satan and the spiritual forces of heaven. Only the second Adam, Jesus of Nazareth, and those united with him (both male and female) by faith and indwelt by his Spirit have such power."[3]

The professor was continually surprised by this student's intellectual maturity and eloquence. However, he had just taken the conversation far above the heads of the rest of the class. Nobody was able to follow where he had just led.

So she reentered the conversation, "These are foundational truths, and they are clearly stated in the narrative, but they have been flatly denied by many of the finest Christian theologians since the second century. As an influential example, let us look at the most important epic in English written by one of the West's finest theologians and poets, John Milton. *Paradise Lost* springs from an almost thoroughly Christian imagination. Milton's ability to fictionalize a Christian worldview creates a masterpiece that goes very far, indeed, in asserting, 'Eternal Providence, / And [justifying] the ways of God to men.'[4]

"Milton takes a pagan form and redeems it at every point (that I can see), but one. He confirms patriarchal paganism's denial of women as equal image-bearers of God who relate to God directly. Males, rather than Christ alone, are made mediators between human beings and their God. Please turn in your books to page 764. Milton has Eve, before the fall, serving her husband before her God. She is "not equal" based on the argument from nature that she doesn't 'seem equal.'

"We move along from line 287 of book 4 consistently with Genesis 1. In Eden Satan recognizes Adam and Eve as together nobler than the other animals. They are both 'God-like erect' with 'native honor' and 'looks divine.' And then, quite out of left field, comes a baldly unbiblical claim.

> Whence true authority in men; though both
> Not equal, as their sex not equal seemed;

3. See Genesis 3:15, Matthew 4:1–11, Colossians 3:10–11.
4. John Milton, *Paradise Lost*, book 1, lines 25–26.

> For contemplation he and valor formed,
> For softness she and sweet attractive grace,
> He for God only, she for God in him;
> His fair large front and eye sublime declared
> Absolute rule . . .[5]

"What follows is then a highly stereotypical definition of masculinity and femininity without any reference to the biblical narrative. Some critics see a reference to 1 Corinthians 11:7–15. Do any of you recognize it?"

Rachel answered, "But that passage gives rationale for how women should pray and prophesy in public, not for how she lives for God through her husband.[6] And I can't remember anywhere in the Scriptures that defines 'masculinity' or 'femininity.'"

Dr. Shaw noticed Matthew, usually so calm and relaxed, getting agitated. He spoke up in an uncharacteristic volume and tone of certainty. "Such a characteristic as Eve's ringleted golden tresses[7] is a mere expression of Milton's racist and patriarchal imagination. Does it mean that my sister in Nigeria is not feminine because she has stiff black hair? It's Pagan myths that define 'masculine' and 'feminine.' And as soon as they do, it is feminine that becomes bad and low. We've seen it in every text we've read. And they do it ad nauseam in our tribal culture. For example, it is insulting to serve a guest beans and corn, because those are feminine foods and so unworthy. You must serve guests yams because they are masculine. And most of our cultural problems stem from our strong patriarchy. FGM, polygamy, wife abuse are big problems that we don't seem to be able to get beyond because we won't give up the masculine superiority that depends upon these definitions.

"The escape from masculine and feminine boxes is a huge attraction to Christianity among my people. Our bishops say they must have women priests to show the people that God can put wisdom in the voice of woman, and the church is about the only place the people hear a woman's voice. Read Chinua Achebe's book *Things Fall Apart* and you will understand our villages in this attitude."

"Yes," said the teacher, "Matthew reminds us that femininity is often more cultural than natural; what seems feminine to one culture (like long,

---

5. Milton, *Paradise Lost*, book 4, 295–300.

6. For a careful explanation of this passage, see Gordon D. Fee's "Praying and Prophesying in the Assemblies," in *Discovering Biblical Equality*, 142–60.

7. See lines 304–10.

blond, waist-length, ringleted hair), may not seem so to another. And the Bible claims applicability in any culture. Some of my friends in Kenya think shaving a woman's hair is feminine because it reduces lice in their husbands' hair.

"Milton gives no logical support for Eve being denied direct relationship with God before the fall. While he does not follow Scripture here, he does follow the church fathers, many early seventeenth-century Puritan divines, and many who deny women's leadership in church and family today.

"Notice how Milton's sole argument is from nature. He tells us Eve is not equal because she doesn't seem equal. Since I have known many very contemplative and valorous women; and I've read about them in the Bible, line 297 does not ring true for me. Milton offers no other reason for his gender distinction than its obviousness. In an argument from nature; one is supposed to just look into the natural world and see the truth of the claim. This type of argument about women was prominent with the church fathers, with the Reformers, and with the gender hierarchicalists of today—even if absent in the Bible.

"If you are interested in the many ways the humanity of women is denied, I suggest an essay by Dorothy Sayers entitled 'Are Women Human?' In 1938 she addressed a women's society and declined to be classified as a 'feminist'.[8] She argued the only really radical and biblical position, that women are human. She did not positively support her claim (for nobody can rationally disagree), but she did show how the humanity of women is continually denied by definitions of gender. I think beginning a discussion of gender by definitions or stereotyping begins unbiblically. The biblical starting place is the common humanity of all people and the principle of diversity within unity. Human beings are primarily a unity, but within the unity is diversity; and the diversity, while not defined, is pronounced 'good.' No individual human ought or wants to be treated primarily according to any sub-class. Unity in Christ is spoiled by divisions according to ethnicity, socioeconomic status, or even the deepest diversity in humanity—gender, for 'All Christians are one in Christ Jesus'[9] according to the Bible."

---

8. Sayers, *Are Women Human?*
9. See Galatians 3:26–29.

Chapter 12

…always giving thanks to God the Father for everything, in the name of our Lord Jesus Christ. Submit to one another out of reverence for Christ.

—Ephesians 5:20–21

During her afternoon office hours that day Ted Mullins came in very agitated to challenge her on her teaching about women in early Genesis. He had a well-founded trust in the biblical teachings and his parental and grandparental authorities that had promoted those convictions. He knew that if he accepted her interpretations in Genesis, he would need to rethink the many New Testament passages based upon them. And if he did that, he could find himself disagreeing for the first time in his life with his relationally successful and biblically based family.

He adored his large extended family, and was poignantly aware that much of their relational success was due to mothers who stayed home and saw the art of homemaking as a high calling from God. He was raised with the idea that service to others was the only path to freedom. His father and all his uncles were spiritual leaders in their own nuclear families and elders in a variety of good Evangelical churches. His father and his uncles and even his grandfathers were all good dads and husbands, and they all deplored what they called "secular feminism." One reason he was proud of them was their commitment to the potential of his sisters and girl cousins, who had all received classical educations with their encouragement. Nora knew she was seriously rattling his cage, and she respected him all the more. She loved the commitment to truth in this young man, and she loved him.

As soon as his bottom hit the student chair in her office, he launched into an excellent summary of what she labeled in her mind as "modified James Hurley." He avoided stereotyping and arguing from nature, the typical complementarian approach, but he maintained the separation of equality of essence and equality of function. The key irritant was, of course, that

Chapter 12

he wanted to be hermeneutically consistent, and knew he wasn't. If he interpreted the first two chapters of Genesis to solidly establish homoousios between men and women as this professor had suggested, how on earth was he going to get to the hierarchy in family and church with which he had been raised?

Professor Shaw listened carefully; and when he was really finished, she asked him, "What contemporary theologian do you trust the most? Who do you think has the most respect for the authority of the Bible?"

Into the L'Abri kitchen of his mind he went. Pulling out drawers and opening cupboards of names in commentaries, books he had read, and who his dad, uncles, and grandfathers referred to as authorities. Finally he answered, "J. I. Packer."

Professor Shaw responded with, "Excellent choice." Then she thought for a moment and reached for a book on her shelf. Ted noted the title was *Standing Forth*.[1] "This is what J. I. Packer says about a theologian called Roger Nicole—Have you ever read Nicole?"

Ted shook his head.

She looked at the front cover and said, "J. I. Packer says Roger Nicole is 'a masterful systematic theologian, poised for logical-exegetical pincer movements against muddles and mistakes.' Pretty high praise from such a man, wouldn't you agree?"

This time Ted nodded his head in agreement.

"I should like to make a deal with you. There is a scholarly essay by Roger Nicole entitled 'In the Beginning There Was Equality' available free online through an organizational website called Christians for Biblical Equality. If you can logically deconstruct, in your essay, even one of Nicole's points in that article, I will give you 100 percent on that paper, no matter what other mistakes may be made. This subject is clearly of deep interest to you, and so I want you to write about it."

He smiled, realizing that she had declined from defending herself, and that she had kept the responsibility for his conclusions soundly in his own lap. He would not ever be able to claim that this professor intellectually coerced, intimidated, or domineered. All she was doing was encouraging him down his own path. "OK," was all he said.

She replied, "You take a dare very courageously."

As he rose and reached for his backpack, she said, "Do you have a minute?"

---

1. Nicole, *Standing Forth*, front cover.

He sat back down nodding his head and raising his shoulders curiously.

She began, "Last time you were in, you said that you still had not decided where to apply for next year. I hesitate to make a suggestion that would certainly be very difficult. Americans are seldom accepted, and it would most certainly not be cheap. But I cannot help but think it a good match for you if it did work out."

Again she had his interest. He asked, "Where are you thinking of?"

"Regent's Park College"

His eyes turned to saucers. "But isn't that one of the Oxford colleges?"

"It is—and a good one, particularly for students with your theological turn of mind and philosophical background. I had a student several years ago in California who reminds me of you in several ways. I wrote his recommendation for Regent's Park, and he ended up being accepted. He did very well there, and is now in a graduate program at Oriel. That student may have earned me credibility with admissions at Regent's Park. And I would be very glad to write a recommendation for you—no matter where you decide to apply. Again, I remind you statistics for Regent's Park are against you. But I think you an excellent candidate for that tutorial program. You and the college would benefit and be benefited. It is an intellectual climate in which I can see you thrive."

"Wow! I never thought of Oxford. But perhaps I should look into it. Thanks for the suggestion."

This time he stood and reached with determination for his backpack. He was now a bloodhound on two scents. He walked out with even more energy than when he entered.

Nora, delighted, sat back in her desk chair, savored the moment, and prayed about Ted's college application process.

She had baited two hooks, and both had gotten bites. The first was far more important. Ted's attitude toward women and most likely a future wife would be strongly influenced by his interpretation of the Genesis passages in question. She was glad that Ted would, no doubt, get feedback from his family in writing his paper. The process of breaking conformity to the world, and of being transformed by the renewing of the mind, though it prove the will of God, was not always comfortable. The support of a loving community was such an advantage, especially to these principled young people. Indeed, she thought, as she remembered the pervasive cynicism among so many of her students, perhaps a loving family was a prerequisite to becoming principled in the first place.

Chapter 12

At moments like this she was filled with prayers of thanksgiving that God had called her into academia. In the polarized world outside the classroom she was often suspect. In churches it was often because she was a woman in academia in the first place. From those circumstances alone she was sometimes considered a "flaming liberal" or a "secular feminist." In other circles, more pro-academic circles, she was suspect for being a Christian in the first place. That label came there with stereotypes of narrow-minded irrationality, bigotry, and judgmentalism. She sometimes wondered if those on the left suspected that she might "proselytize" rather than teach, and that those on the right suspected that she might teach and ignore "sharing the gospel."

But Nora was hired to teach literature, and that is precisely what she wanted to do. It was the texts themselves that she longed to open to students. By helping students understand and interpret the ideas contained therein, she plunged them into the battle for truth. And that was her calling. The texts spoke for themselves, and open, uncensored, respectful conversations about those texts enamored her with academia. As her culture polarized, her beloved academic freedom was being threatened from both left and right. But in her classroom and office, people were free to say what they thought, and people who disagreed could honestly and respectfully challenge them. Os was always promoting what he called "The Civil Public Square."[2] She often thought her square classroom was just such a square. Her students were invited to say what they really thought, but they were also accountable to texts, reason and civility for supporting what they said.

She had been criticized in Christian circles for treating the Bible just like any other book, and in hermeneutical terms that was true in her classroom. She used the same principles of interpretation with the Bible as she did with other texts. She believed the Bible was inerrant and authoritative, but the only solid foundation for these conclusions was understanding the Bible first as a book, as one understands other books.

Dr. Schaeffer always used to say, "The only reason to believe anything, is because you are convinced it is true with a capital 'T.'" It seemed to her it was God's business to convince, and hers to simply teach what the text was saying. She did this with the Bible as with all the books on her syllabus. "What does the text mean?" was the question guiding her pedagogy, no matter what they were reading. In her devotional life, the truth and authority of the Bible were a source of life and the light to her path. In her classroom, the truth and authority of the Bible were claims the text made about itself.

2. Guinness, *Case for Civility*.

Chapter 13

Pure and undefiled religion before God and the Father is this: to visit orphans and widows in their trouble, and to keep oneself unspotted from the world.

—JAMES 1:27

THE TWO OFFICE HOURS had not been busy. Crystal was absent on Monday because of the flu, so Nora had given her a make-up quiz on "Hymn to Aten" and Egyptian love poetry. Servat had come in to discuss the essay she was writing on a comparison between Jesus in the Christian gospels and in the *Qu'ran*. Lastly, Travis Williams had come in with a few questions about how he would support his claim that the Santorini eruption was the source of Hesiod's Titanomachy. Dana came in with a few MLA documentation questions. Nora looked at her watch as she closed her office door. She was in good time to make her meeting at Promise.

Exiting Avery Hall she advanced across Avery Mall, still white with snow. The sidewalks were cleared, and her boots crunched salt against concrete. The world must, indeed, seem cold and hard to Jill Kelly.

Nora questioned how she could possibly understand this poor woman well enough to be helpful. She was no professional therapist. What if she said something damaging? She recognized the attack, and began praying.

"Lord, help me be a blessing to this girl through your power. In myself I cannot do it. Fill me with your love that it may wash over this fragile young woman. Make me a firm and dependable friend. Grant me wise questions and delayed advice. Help me to really hear. Employ me for healing and comfort. And, most loving of fathers, please take this affliction and use it for her inner growth and edification; protect her from its potential for permanent devastation. Make something beautiful from the ugliness. Please, Father, draw her to yourself and bless her with the filling of your comforter. Amen."

Chapter 13

Nora shored up her confidence by telling herself, "I can be a conduit for God's love; I can listen; I can ask questions; and I can be present. Perhaps this is what she will need from me."

Rounding the corner of the Belk Library, Nora emerged onto Howard Street. By the time she had passed Raley and Depot Street, only a bit more than a block later, the cold was penetrating the down in her jacket and the flesh on her bones. She could now see the crisis pregnancy center. From the street it looked low and narrow, its stone front incognito among the other old downtown buildings. But Nora saw it as a key battlefield in the spiritual war, an important place, like her classroom, where cultural lies were exposed. Here exploited women and unwanted children received provision, support and love, the nuclear weapon in this war.

Nora tugged hard to open the door against the wind. As soon as it was ajar enough to catch the wind, it blew open with such violence that Nora was almost knocked over. "The Spirit's power," she thought as she left the cold and hard and entered the warm and gentle. "This is the zeitgeist of ecumenical Christianity and a milieu of my faith in which I belong. For here I can relate and serve."

Mae was looking at an opened file drawer behind the receptionist's desk when Nora entered the foyer. She turned from her reading with an amiable and appreciative smile. "I'm so glad you've come. The more I get to know Jill, the more I'm convinced this is a good client-mentor match. Jill is waiting back in my office; come on in." Nora followed Mae down the hall.

As she walked in and first saw Jill, Nora thought of Chesterton's definition of "wood: the most human of non-human things."[1] For Jill was all wood-browns. Her large, deep-browed walnut eyes contrasted beautifully with the honey oak of her skin. Her shoulder-length mahogany hair waved like the grain Nora remembered in her grandmother's piano. Nora received Jill's tentative outstretched right hand firmly in both her own and met her with a profoundly welcoming smile. Jill began to relax.

Mae articulated the policies and expectations for the relationship that had been discussed in the mentoring class, and which, she was sure, Jill had also heard before. When the introductory stuff seemed complete, Nora said, "I saw, when I walked past Expresso Yosef, that it was almost empty. Jill, may I get you a cup of coffee?"

Jill and Nora said their thank-yous and good-byes to Mae, stepped out again into the cold and hard for only a few minutes, then entered another

---

1. Chesterton, "Wood," in *Universe according to G. K. Chesterton*, ed. Ahlquist.

kind of haven. They were greeted by the aroma of roasting coffee beans and the faint whirr of frothing milk. Stepping into a good coffeehouse on a cold day was one of the joys of life. A glance at Jill's approving smile assured Nora that she felt the same. They both ordered a latte and then carried them upstairs. The little conversation area where they landed had seen better days. Decorated in a style that might be called "Student Thrift Store," the space was private and comfortable with a view of Howard Street below. Droves of students, tucked as far inside their jackets as they could manage, hurried toward warm dormitories, apartments, libraries, dining commons, and restaurants. But Jill and Nora were a world away from the bustle outside, even if only separated by panes of glass. Jill was taking time to ease into being still and together. Nora held her latte with both hands in front of her face, the better to savor it with the most senses, and to communicate to Jill that she was contentedly parked. Nothing was said for several minutes. The relationship had no history, so the "nothing" meant nothing in the way.

Jill broke the comfortable silence with, "Thanks for doing this for me."

Nora said, "My own daughter is in California. I wish I could sit with her and have a private chat about her troubles. Perhaps you'll be the one who is good for me."

Jill's responsive smile read, "Unconvinced."

Nora asked, "What are you studying?"

"I am an Interior Design major. But I don't have tons of professional ambition. I mean, I really wanted to come to university because I love learning, and because I love interior design. I thought it was something that I could do along with raising a family. If I was doing something high powered, I might have to send my kids off to daycare . . . Well, maybe that sort of thinking isn't relevant anymore."

Nora continued, "Mae told me that your pregnancy was forced upon you, and yet that you have decided to carry the child to term. I respect that."

"I don't suppose it's the baby's fault. Why should the baby be killed for the father's crime? . . . I feel so ashamed already; to do away with my own child would simply make me even more ashamed of myself."

Nora interjected, "I don't suppose it's your fault either; and the decision took courage."

"Maybe, but I don't question that abortion would have been wrong for me. I was raised in a Christian family that always taught me that human life has a sacred dignity, whether convenient or not. I'm discovering now that I just accepted many things I was taught on authority simply because

Chapter 13

I trusted my parents. But for the sanctity of human life I have many good reasons to believe. Besides, it's so good to have at least something I'm morally clear about right now. I wish I was clear about what to do after the birth . . . Mae has arranged for me to meet with a woman from the adoption agency on Friday."

"How do you feel about that?"

"Most of the time I'm convinced I should give the child to a stable, loving family that really wants a baby now; and I know it would feel good to have actually identified such a family."

"And the rest of the time?"

"The rest of the time I just want to love my own baby and trust God to take care of the both of us. But then I think such thoughts are just proof of my irresponsibility. Financially, I can't even take care of myself; how can I take care of somebody else? If I don't finish school, how will I ever be financially independent?"

"Do you have the support of your family? How do they fit in this picture?"

"My mom has been as good about this as I had hoped. She's not pressuring me, and I know she'll be there for me. Her tagline is, 'Prayerfully take one step at a time.' But my mom is not the one who makes the decisions in our family. And I'm not really sure what my dad is thinking or feeling—other than disappointment. My due date is well after spring finals, so he has said that he thinks I should finish out this year, and then . . . 'We'll see.' I sometimes wonder if he's really glad he did such a good job of teaching me that abortion was wrong. And I wish I didn't suspect that part of the reason he's so eager for me to finish out the year is so he doesn't have to take his round-bellied, unmarried daughter off to church on Sundays. His tagline was always, 'It's a fallen world.' But I think he's discovering that he cherished visions of the contrary. I know he's reeling from the fact that this has happened to his family.

"I usually talk to my sister, Katie, on the weekends; she's very understanding, but very busy with her classes at Chapel Hill. Her boyfriend, Darren, is my friend Holly's brother. So he realizes that it could have been Holly with my problem. He's supportive of Katie, me, and Holly. My brother Trevor doesn't even consider that I might not keep the baby; he's so eager to be an uncle. My youngest brother, Brandon, doesn't really get what's happened. My parents are waiting to see what I decide before they thoroughly explain things to him."

During a lull in the conversation Nora remembered that at the first meeting mentors were supposed to make sure clients understood the basics of the physical changes pregnancy brought upon their bodies and to reassure the client of strict confidentiality. After a statement of commitment to confidentiality, Nora queried into the biological subject. Jill's answers showed her to have been listening well in her biology classes. She was a bright, well-educated young woman.

When Nora had satisfied herself on that physical score, she returned the talk to the emotional side of Jill's support system and asked, "How is your relationship with the other girls who were involved? Don't you live with them?"

Jill sighed and exhaled deeply, as though the very mention of Holly and Megan released tension. "I could not have survived this without them. We have gone through this, so far, really together. One of the reasons I told Mae I wanted to talk with you is so I wouldn't burden them too much. They have so much to work through themselves; I didn't think they needed to be constantly hearing about what I'm going to do about this pregnancy. They both are against abortion, and supported me on that decision. Holly wants to be a nurse-midwife and is fascinated with the whole birthing thing; she'll coach me through the birth. I know Holly feels responsible for all of us going to the frat party in the first place, and it will be good for her to help me in that way. If I'm going to let the baby be adopted, I don't want my mom to go through the birth with me. I know she would bond with the baby—No sense in both of us having that agony. Megan's a rock of a friend. Holly and Megan are seeing a therapist since they told their parents about the frat party. My parents wanted me to go to one, but I didn't want to. Maybe I'll need to go if I give the baby up for adoption."

Jill seemed very open, so Nora dared ask, "Do you think there is any area where you are afraid about healing besides coping with adoption?" Jill immediately tensed up, and Nora was afraid she had gone too far too soon.

But Jill still spoke on. "Yeah, I've got a real problem about speaking to guys. I haven't talked to a single guy my age since it happened. Yesterday my freshman comp teacher had us get with a partner to peer edit a draft of an essay. I was sitting next to a perfectly nice guy, and everybody else around us was already paired up. So we exchanged papers. I couldn't get the thought out of my head that this could have been one of the guys in the frat house. I made editing notes on his paper, but I couldn't say a word. A few times he asked me questions about how I was following his argument, but

Chapter 13

I couldn't say a word. I just sat there without looking at him. I was soooo weird. He must think I'm a total jerk.

"I really wish that detective would tell us that they've arrested whoever did it. Then I wouldn't wonder about every guy I meet. If a guy asks me a question, I'll nod or shake my head. Sometimes I'll lift my shoulders to show that I don't know the answer. But I haven't said a word to any guy near my age except my brother."

"Are you so sure you are uncomfortable with every young man?"

"I am surrounded by strange guys all day long on campus, and if any of them so much as seems like they intend to give me any sort of attention at all, I freak out on the inside."

Nora commented, "Well, when that feeling fades, we'll know you're healing significantly. And I'm sure it will fade. I'd like you to keep me updated on that problem."

Jill's brief nod was one of shameful agreement. "A few weeks ago I went to an InterVarsity large-group meeting. I noticed a guy there who seemed especially kind. I overhead him talking to his friends, and it gave me the impression that he was indeed a good friend. Maybe I'll try to talk to him."

"Are there any other things you're doing or not doing that might reflect some unhealthy ways of coping?"

Following a pause of consideration Jill responded with, "Yeah, I easily run too much. I've always loved running, but now it's the only time that I actually feel good. After an hour or so of hammering, I get a refreshing high. Last Saturday I couldn't give it up. I ran about twenty miles. I shouldn't be going that far without training for it. I haven't done a marathon in two years. As this pregnancy progresses, I need to be content with a modest swim."

Nora agreed. "I think you're right. I'll bet Holly and Megan have some new quirks going."

"I'll say. Holly hardly does anything but study and eat. She says eating proves that she has control over what goes into her body, and studying is the only thing that keeps her mind from dwelling on what happened. She also says that she will never date again, and she no longer intends to marry. I wonder whether she'll ever be able to trust a guy again . . . I sometimes wish I had her quirks. When I study, it's more the opposite. I can't seem to concentrate; and when I do learn something, I easily forget it. My quiz grades have gone down . . . And I can't so easily give up the idea of getting married. I've always dreamed of marriage and kids, but how can you have that without trusting a man?"

Nora replied, "You're right; trust is an essential ingredient for a good marriage, but it is something that may return with your healing. How you feel now will likely not be how you feel in five years. What about Megan?"

Megan seems totally fine during the week, but she's been tempted to drink ever since it happened. Saturday night before last, she went out with some girls from the second floor and came back totally plastered. She was really sick all night. She begged us not to tell her parents. We said we wouldn't if it never happened again and if she told her therapist all about it. She did, and she's been OK ever since. But I worry about her . . . I think it would be easier for them if I hadn't gotten pregnant—It's such a constant reminder of the reality of something none of us even remembers. It would be so easy to treat the frat party like some sort of nightmare from which we have awakened—If I wasn't pregnant . . . But I am, and I don't know what to do about it."

Following a caesura Nora commented, "You were given clear guidance about the abortion. Why not take your mother's sound advice and prayerfully take the next step when required."

"I don't suppose I can offer a better answer."

"I would like to tell you something from my experience; how relevant it is, I don't know. But there have been several times in my life when I knew I was following and pleasing God, and that at each of those times I received accusations of being irresponsible. I think it likely that whatever decision you make about the child, somebody will think you are irresponsible. Even though I have known you only a short while, I am convinced that whether you choose parenting or adoption, it will not be an irresponsible choice."

Nora glanced at her watch and said, "I have a class in about twenty minutes. I should go soon, but I think we should meet as soon after your talk with the adoption agency as is convenient for you. Do you have any time next Tuesday afternoon?"

"My last class is over at 3:50. I could be here by four."

"That will work fine for me as well. I look forward to seeing you soon."

As Nora rose and reached for her backpack, she noticed Jill wasn't stirring. And she wore a very puzzled expression. Nora asked, "Have I said something that upset you?"

Bewildered, Jill said, "Mae told me you were an older mother; she didn't tell me you were a grad student."

Chapter 13

Nora smiled wide. "Mae is right on both counts. I'm sixty, which always classifies as older when compared to nineteen, but, I might add, seems younger as time flies. And I am not only a mother, but a grandmother. I'm afraid you are the one mistaken; I am an English professor here."

Jill's astonished, "You are?" made Nora smile again.

"I hope that doesn't make you rethink becoming a friend of mine. Do you have a particular beef against English professors?"

"No. I think it's really cool that you have time for me . . . And I love to read."

"Everybody's time is valuable. And developing a good relationship is one way of spending it wisely. If you enjoy reading, we'll never run out of interesting things to talk about . . . I really do hope your meeting on Friday goes well."

As Jill's confusion cleared, she said, "Thanks so much, bye."

"See you Tuesday."

Chapter 14

It is time to effect a revolution in female manners—time to restore to them their lost dignity—and make them, as a part of the human species, labour by reforming themselves to reform the world. It is time to separate unchangeable morals from local manners.

—MARY WOLLSTONECRAFT, *A VINDICATION OF THE RIGHTS OF WOMAN*

OUT ON HOWARD STREET Nora turned left into the cold wind and headed back toward the center of campus. She focused on the background, the beautiful dome of the Belk Library. It was a pulse of her new life, literally and experientially a high point. Before she knew the area well, she had used it to orient herself and keep from getting lost. But her research there helped her not get lost intellectually as well. She went there for facts and ideas, for beautiful expression and knowledge itself. She often thought of it as a gold mine. When she was inside, she pursued veins of thought, sorting through and casting aside quantities of irrelevant rubble to expose the pure nuggets of knowledge relevant for her life and work. In front of the Belk Library she turned right and went down two sets of stairs to Anne Belk Hall.

The English Department had long since outgrown Avery Hall. Every semester poor Tim Furniston, their departmental assistant, had to scrounge classrooms wherever he could find them available at the times needed. This semester she had a modern world literature class in Anne Belk among the history classes.

This afternoon students would finish discussing and have a reading quiz on the Kenyan novel *The River Between*, by Ngugi Wa Thiong'o. It was a book she loved, but she was having trouble transitioning from the conversation in the coffee house to the one coming up in the classroom.

She thought, as she often did in such circumstances, "All truth is God's, so all things are related. How is Jill's situation like Nyambura's?" It was an easy question, for both suffered from sins rooted in patriarchy. Jill's rape was a premiere example of the pejorative "ruling over" part of the curse in Genesis 3. An act, especially when premeditated, that was more about the male gaining a sense of power through domination of the female than about lust for sex. It was as culturally prevalent as it was illegal. The last statistic she read claimed one in every four women on American university campuses had been sexually assaulted. She thought of the place of pornography in her own culture and the dehumanization of women in advertising. She thought of the low view of marriage and the acceptance of adultery and divorce. All these plagues seemed related to not loving women as equals, a concept she considered basic to a Christian world view.

But how can the results of patriarchy be confronted without confronting the sin of patriarchy itself? Her friend Dominic Misolo in Kenya had pointed out the basic fallacy of this common thinking in the church. It is as inefficient an attack upon sin in contemporary American Christianity as it was among the new Kikuyu Christians along the Honia. The church's euphemistic "servant leadership," which really means excluding women from leadership in home and church, unintentionally allows for an epidemic of verbal abuse in the home and sexual harassment in the church as consistently as Kikuyu patriarchy allowed for polygamy and female circumcision.

During the lecture Dr. Shaw asks the class, "What were the patriarchal cultural practices that the missionaries condemned in Kikuyu culture?"

A voice from the right said, "Female circumcision, polygamy, and wife beating."

"Right, and what biblical evidence did they give to support their condemnation?"

A voice from the left said, "The book didn't give any biblical argument. It just said that the missionaries were horrified and called the practices 'barbaric.' That only really means that they were shocked because they weren't used to it in their own culture."

From the front came, "By just calling it barbaric, the missionaries threatened the dignity of Kikuyu people, alienating them when they wanted them to become Christians. They should have explained why these things were wrong from the Bible."

Dr. Shaw asked, "Where in the Bible does it condemn female circumcision?" and looked out on thirty-five blank faces.

She tries again, "How did Waiyaki respond to the gospel from the missionaries?"

Again from the right, "At first he was very sympathetic. He didn't like circumcision either, especially after Muthoni died. He even liked what the missionaries were saying because it challenged what he didn't approve in his own culture. He loved the basic gospel, and he loved the literacy they brought."

"What alienated him from the Christians?"

"It was when they got all legalistic on him. For example they, both the British missionaries and the Kikuyu believers, said he couldn't go to school at Siriana if he was circumcised."

"Why did they become more legalistic?"

This time from the back of the room, "They made the rules because they had been trying and trying to get them to stop the circumcisions. And they wouldn't stop."

"Why wouldn't they stop?"

The same voice from the back answered, "They wouldn't stop because it was a deeply ingrained cultural tradition that defined masculine and feminine. Muthoni knew she couldn't get married and have a family in that culture if she wasn't circumcised. She thought she had to be circumcised to be fully female."

A new voice popped the question, "I can't understand why they thought this. If you get your clitoris chopped off, and sometimes worse, you're less, not more, of a woman."

Another female voice near the center responded with, "I think the problem is that they didn't think like that. They just believed what their patriarchal culture said because the missionaries didn't teach them a biblical equality. Because the Bible doesn't talk specifically about female circumcision, they needed to know the biblical principle of equality. The missionaries themselves didn't know that principle applied to people; they only applied it to the Trinity with fancy words like "homoousios." In terms of patriarchy, Nyambura was no better off than Muthoni. Joshua and Livingstone seem just as patriarchal as Chege. Only Waiyaki seems willing to question patriarchy, at least a little."

Dr. Shaw says, "Indeed, Waiyaki is willing to accept the basics of the Christian gospel, but Wa Thiong'o writes: 'For Waiyaki knew that not all the ways of the white man were bad. Even his religion was not essentially bad. Some good, some truth shone through it. But the religion, the faith, needed washing.' What do you think Waiyaki and/or Wa Thiong'o himself thought needed washing out of the Christianity of the missionaries?"

Chapter 14

"Patriarchy," came immediately from three female voices at once.

"Legalism," piped up a Christian in the corner.

"Racism," came soundly from a black student on the right.

"The forcing of British imperial culture," interposed a cultural geography major on the left.

Dr. Shaw replied, "Yes, I see textual evidence for all those suggestions . . . None of you proposed a dependence upon literacy as needing 'washing out' of the missionaries influence upon Kikuyu culture. But we've talked about the rich oral culture they enjoyed before the missionaries' arrival, and the traditional wisdom of their elders was contained in their own proverbs and maxims. The elders seemed content to remain illiterate. Can you explain their immediate embrace of literacy even before their embrace of Christianity?"

The cultural geography major provided the observation that all the good leaders in the novel respected knowledge and truth for its own sake, and they recognized that knowledge could be gained through the written word. She said, "Men like Chege understood that they needed to know what was written to understand their new reality. I don't think Chege wanted to learn to read. But he did want his son to learn so that someone he trusted could tell him what the writing meant. He knew that, because the writing meant something, he was excluded from knowing something. If the missionaries cared about communicating the gospel, they should have cared about understanding the people and culture they were speaking into. Just knowing the tribe's mythology wasn't sinful in their own view, but believing in it. The missionaries could have learned the Kikuyu stories without worshipping their gods. And regardless of the spiritual side of things, many Kikuyu proverbs contained practical wisdom which could have been especially helpful to the missionaries in their new environment. By acknowledging that wisdom, the missionaries would have been expressing respect for the people."

Dr. Shaw responded with, "You are grappling with this text. Your interpretations are mature and insightful . . . I wonder why Joshua was able to reject circumcision without rejecting patriarchy?"

The black student on the right posited, "Because Joshua was one of the first converts, it's like he already had to make an almost total break with his culture. He was already a tribal outsider; perhaps it was easier for him to be critical of the culture that had rejected him."

Dr. Shaw asked, "Did Joshua reject his culture, or just some of its practices? He seems to care for his people, doesn't he?"

"Yea, I think he really does care for them. Maybe I want to say that he's willing to do what he thinks is right without their approval because he was used to having their disapproval," came the modified answer. "And if his new religion really was more loving, maybe he was more sensitive to the women's sufferings, even though he was still a rule-the-roost sort of guy."

A woman in the front row said, "I don't think he was really more loving than the pagans. Look at how quickly he disowns his own daughters. His opposition to female circumcision and polygamy seems more about his own self-righteousness than love for his daughters or other women of the tribe. Being a rule-the-roost sort of guy is essentially asserting one's superiority. Patriarchy by definition denies love and devalues relationship. I know I'm glad he's not my dad or husband."

Dr. Shaw asks, "Isn't it possible to see one's supposed higher place in a hierarchy as merely a responsibility for service? . . . A 'restless lies the head that wears a crown' sort of syndrome?"

Now the Christian in the corner spoke up again, "The curse in Genesis 3:16 predicts that all men after the fall will want to dominate women. Patriarchy just gives them on a silver platter the opportunities to abuse women. Before the fall Adam was thrilled that he had someone on his own level and that she was a different gender. Patriarchy says, 'I have a right to boss women around.' Sometimes a man uses that to do what's best for her, but it's like slavery. Some slave owners treated their slaves well, but the best slave owners set their slaves free. They didn't hang on to the corrupting power of illegitimate control. It's also similar to Livingstone's assumption of priority. If he thought the gospel was true, he was serving the Kikuyu by bringing it to them. But the temptation lies in using that position to dominate the tribe. When he gave their land away to other whites, he acted illegitimately. He had no more right to say that white trumps black than for men to say that male trumps female. And in a fallen world authority without accountability easily becomes 'normal' abuse, and selflessness the exception. Joshua reflected real Christianity in his acceptance of the gospel and in his subjection of cultural practices to biblical authority as he understood it, not in how he thought about ruling-the-roost. He should have listened to Miriamu, who was more Christian than Joshua, because she was more loving."

"It sounds to me as though many of you have understood this novel very well and have many opinions about it. You might consider a thesis from this text for your next essay. Many of these claims you have made in our discussion today could use textual support.

Chapter 14

"I hate to break off our discussion, but you do need to take the reading quiz before you leave. Over the weekend you will begin our next work which is from the other side of Africa. Chinua Achebe's *Things Fall Apart* is set in Nigeria; it also deals with the challenges Christianity brought to tribal life. You will encounter similar, if not more severe patriarchy, in Igbo culture. Cultural definitions of masculine and feminine continue as an important element of pagan culture, and one with which Achebe is particularly concerned. We will begin our discussion of *Things Fall Apart* on Monday. I'll pass out your quiz now on *The River Between*, and you may leave when you are satisfied with its completion."

Chapter 15

As a father pities his children,
So the Lord pities those who fear him.

—Psalm 103: 13

Tuesday dawned sunny and clear, if brisk. After office hours Nora headed down Howard Street, praying for Jill as she went. Since meeting her last week, Jill had become a constant presence in Nora's consciousness. She remembered telling Luke about how much she liked and respected Jill. In California Luke had been on the board of directors for the local crisis pregnancy center and was particularly interested in that kind of ministry. He wanted to know all about her mentoring at Promise. He had significant counseling background, and Nora regarded him as an important resource in her relationship with Jill. Over the years Luke and Nora had developed an ability to thoroughly talk over caregiving experiences without sacrificing confidentiality. Luke did not know Jill's name or any biographical "facts" about her, but he did know that she had a living relationship with her Savior, that she was mature beyond her years, that she was very self-aware, that she was struggling with the adoption decision, and that her relationship with Nora was off on a good footing. Luke prayed for Nora's Promise mentee with and without Nora.

At four o'clock Nora opened the door to Expresso Yosef and thrilled to the scent of warm coffee beans just taken from the roaster. After picking up a cup of decaf and stirring in some half and half, she climbed the stairs. There was Jill, already ensconced in the chair she sat in at their last meeting and sipping at her unbleached paper cup with its corrugated cardboard ring. But Jill's countenance was radically different. She bore a look of triumph. Her welcoming smile did not flow from the heart of a victim. Nora knew at once that a corner had been turned and that Jill was eager to tell a story.

Chapter 15

Subsequent to brief, but genuinely friendly greetings, Nora asked how the meeting with the adoption agent had gone. The narrative of an important weekend gushed forth.

"Friday night I was a disaster. Mrs. Doyle from the agency in Asheville was really nice. She was super respectful of me and my situation. She had a whole notebook of responsible, loving, Christian families who want to adopt. My conviction that adoption is a good and beautiful option was strengthened, and yet it only made me feel worse for not wanting it for my baby and myself. I was an emotional mess. I couldn't eat that night. I couldn't talk about it with Megan or Holly because I didn't know what to say. I went to bed with a splitting headache before calling my mom like I'd promised her, and I couldn't sleep. As I lay there stewing, I prayed, 'Lord, I'll do whatever you want me to do with this baby, but please show me clearly what you want me to do.' It was like a spring inside me began to unwind. I began to relax, and I fell asleep.

"In the morning my Bible reading schedule directed me to Psalm 127. God spoke to me in verse 3 and put the whole dilemma in a new light. 'Behold, children are a heritage from the Lord, / The fruit of the womb is a reward.' I had been thinking of the 'fruit of the womb' as a responsibility, as a burden, as a human being entirely dependent upon me—not as a reward. I had been so afraid that if I kept the baby, I might blame the baby or that the baby would continually remind me of that horrible crime against myself. I realized that deep down a suspicion lurked that God was punishing me for something. God's Word did not change my circumstances, but it revolutionized how I interpreted them.

"This child within me is not just a biological consequence of a rape, he or she is a reward for me from God. I did not turn away from him in my worst trauma, and I am now convinced that he has chosen to bless me for that. What the frat boys meant for evil, God has turned to good. If God intends to reward me with this baby, then it is not irresponsible to trust him to care for us both.

"Saturday morning I just thanked him for his gift of life, and prayed that he would begin to show me how things could work out.

"Not five minutes after praying that, Holly and Megan came back from the McGinn. They sat down beside me and Megan said, 'We've been talking about the possibility of you keeping the baby. It's totally up to you, and we'll support you in whatever you decide. But we want you to know that if you decide to keep the baby, we will do whatever we can to help you. If we had that baby to love, we feel we could get on better. We have both thought about our academic schedules, and we could both register for Monday, Wednesday, Friday classes from now on. If you could take Tuesday/Thursday classes, Holly and I could each take care of the baby one day a week.'

Holly added, 'We don't want to pressure you; we just want you to know that we would love your baby and that we think we would heal by helping you.' We all just cried and hugged."

By this time Nora was herself in tears. She asked herself, "Why am I so surprised that when I try to be a blessing to someone, I am the one blessed? It happens every time."

"Saturday afternoon my parents called. Usually I talk to my mom most of the time. But my dad seemed to need to talk. He told me that he's been thinking about his on-campus policy, as he calls it. He's always told us kids that if we kept up good grades and wanted to go to college, he would pay four years of tuition, books, dorm room, and meals. He's always said that he would not pay for cars, off-campus housing, or any luxuries.

"But he said, 'If you really want to keep your baby, I would pay what I'm paying now for your dorm room for an off-campus apartment. And I would be willing to give you as much grocery money as I'm now spending for your meal account. The price of tuition and books won't change, so it may be possible for you to survive in school with a child. I really don't know. But I just felt led to tell you that I'd be willing to support you off campus for the same amount.'"

Through a teary smile Jill said, "I've never felt so much appreciation for my dad in my life . . . I am very sure that God is confirming to me that I should parent my own child, and I am so happy about it. I'm very aware that things will not be easy, but I'm now certain that I will love my baby and that God will help me take good care of him or her."

Nora, barely able to speak through her emotion, said, "I am so happy also. You are already an excellent mother, and in God you have the best of helpers. Thank you so much for entrusting me with your beautiful story."

"I'm not done. After I talked with my dad, I told Holly and Megan that I had decided to keep the baby. They were so glad. The first thing they did, after I told them what my dad said, was call home. They told their folks that I wanted to keep the baby and move off campus next year. They asked if their parents would make a similar deal with them as my dad did with me. Their parents agreed! They said that if we could find a place for the three of us, on the AppalCart route, for no more than they are paying now, Holly

Chapter 15

and Megan could live off campus too. With the three of us sharing rent, we may be able to find a place we can afford."

Nora enthusiastically affirmed the wisdom of the plan, and expressed that she hoped they could find such a place.

Jill said, "I have another good thing to tell you."

Nora responded, "How is that possible? You've shared so much good news already."

"Well you said to tell you if I talked to any guys, and I did. After the large-group IV meeting, the guy I told you about last time was working at the refreshment table. He asked me if I wanted some tea. I said, 'Yes, thanks.' I know it's not a lengthy oration, but it's a start. He just smiled and handed me a cup. And the strangest thing was that I was comfortable. There was no panic inside."

Nora exclaimed, "Wonderful, that is sound progress. I'm certain real conversations are on the horizon. Good for you."

For some time they just enjoyed their coffee and what had just passed between them. Then Nora asked, "I'm glad some hopes for the near future are beginning to come into focus. I'm wondering how they are different from the hopes you imagined last summer before you came to Blue Ridge?"

Jill replied, "It feels like everything about my future has changed. I've always wanted to be a homemaker. A main reason I chose my major, interior design, was because I envisioned that it was something I could do with kids. I didn't want a super-stressful profession that would mean daycare for my kids. I've always dreamed of being home with them. I have never wanted a frantically busy lifestyle in which I always had to juggle time with my kids. That dream, of course, presupposed that I'd have a husband with a profession. All the single moms I've known are champion jugglers—I'll need to learn juggling.

"The most important thing I'm really having trouble letting go of, though, is the idea that my child won't have a father. It makes me very sad, and makes me question whether my child can really grow up emotionally healthy. I just can't think that there is anything more important for a child than to know that his or her mother and father love each other and that together they love him or her. And that is just what I can never give my child."

Nora asked, "Are you really so sure of that?"

With low volume and high passion, Jill yelled at Nora. "I don't even know who my child's father is, and I hate him! He hates me, or he would never have abused me so. I HATE him!"

83

The anger was bitter and intense, but Nora knew it was not directed at her. She calmly nodded her head, hoping Jill would sense that she had been heard and understood—that Nora had accepted some of Jill's burden and that it was OK with Nora if Jill lost emotional control. After a few more sympathetic nods, Nora said, "Your feelings are rational and understandable." Words like "unforgiving" or "right" were conspicuously absent and so were heard by this very sensitive young woman. And both women returned seriously to the sipping of coffee.

Later Nora asked how Holly and Megan were doing.

Jill replied, "Holly is still tempted to overeat, but she noticed last week that the meal account on her BlueridgeCard has a dangerously low balance. She realizes that if she's not going to starve at the end of the semester, she'll need to eat less now. She's also coming swimming most days with Megan and me. But going swimming is almost the only thing she does beside eat, sleep, attend classes, and study. She says she needs top grades from her BS in nursing to get into a good midwife program after Blue Ridge, and she really loves all that biological stuff. Her homework really is obsessive, but I think it's working for her. I suppose there is a worse coping mechanism than getting straight A's."

"How's Megan doing?"

"Well, she hasn't gone out drinking again. She said last night that she's so excited about the baby that she has something really great to look forward to. She said, 'I don't want to be a drunken aunt.' I think she's doing much better. Her grades have also dipped, but we're both at least still passing all our classes. She likes her church in Poplar, and she goes to Catholic Campus Ministry meetings. She went there her first week at Blue Ridge, so she knew her friends there before the frat party. I think she's told the CCM minister about everything. I'm certain CCM is really helping her."

Nora said, "All of you are doing amazingly well. You seem so good for each other. It would be quite normal to be making stupid and damaging decisions right now. You all appear willing to allow God to help you through—by his means . . . except perhaps one. You acknowledge the importance of church community for Megan. What about you and Holly? Why don't you two go to church? Didn't you say that your families went to the same church in your hometown?"

For the first time, Nora detected defensiveness in Jill's answer. "We're going to IV together."

Chapter 15

Nora said, "An excellent choice—However, I know Shane Sayers, the campus minister for IV, so I know that he is advising you to plug into a local church as soon as possible. Why would you want to go to IV, but not a church?"

Jill was not at all caught off guard by the question. She, and Nora assumed Holly too, had carefully considered it for some time. "IV has a high view of the Scriptures. We have good Bible study and worship there. But IV is also egalitarian. At IV you don't get a bunch of stuff about men's roles and women's roles. They don't go in for stereotyping at IV, and they don't preach patriarchy. We even heard a woman give a sermon at large-group.

"Holly and I decided last summer that we wouldn't go to church in Poplar unless we heard about one that had both a high view of Scripture and treated women like regular people."

Nora's response seemed lame even to herself. "Some churches harp on the subject more than others; couldn't you go to one that doesn't mention the subject very often and admit you have a minor difference of theology?"

Again the clarity of Jill's response reflected reflection. "No, we couldn't. We're afraid that we'll meet our future spouse at church. We read some pretty amazing statistics about how many single people fall in love with somebody at their church. We decided it wasn't worth the risk. If you attend a church that believes in patriarchy, especially one that keeps the subject under the rug, one of us could end up married to a bossy guy and not realize it until it was too late. We don't want marriages like our parents."

Jill's answer brought the obvious question "What are your parents' marriages like?" to Nora's mind. But their relationship was so new, and she had no idea what it would cause to surface. She rejected such a direct question. So she suggested, "And Megan doesn't think like you and Holly on this subject? I have known some fairly patriarchal Catholics."

Jill's, "Megan thinks exactly like us, but her dad is perfect in that way," made Nora question for the first time Jill's logical connection.

"I'm not sure I understand you."

"When Megan was born, her dad, Dr. Colin Clery, was the principal of the big Catholic High School in Charlotte, St. James. Her real mom had been a French teacher there, but she took a long maternity leave to stay home and take care of Megan. But after the birth, Megan's mom didn't seem to recover well. She got really tired and needed a lot of help from Dr. Clerytaking care of Megan. When Megan was nine months old, they discovered that her mom had pancreatic cancer. She died two days after Megan's first birthday."

"Oh, how tragic," sighed Nora.

"But not the next bit—Dr. Clery really loved his wife, and he really loves Megan—And he quit his great job at St. James, so he could take care of them himself. He sold the bigger house they used to own before her mom passed away and bought a real small place next door to Megan's grandparents. Because of getting the cheaper house and selling one of their cars, he didn't have to work for three years. He stayed home and took care of Megan until she was old enough to go to the preschool at their church. When Dr. Clery went back to St. James, it was like he had to start his career all over again. He went back as a PE teacher for freshman guys because it was the only job opening. He went from the top of the pecking order to the bottom. And it really didn't bother him. He just said things like, 'Administration comes with some headaches, and I love kids and teaching.'

"My dad, Robert Kelly, and Holly's dad, Vernon Billingham, are Dr. Clery's friends, and they disapproved. They still say that he should have kept his job and let Megan's grandmother and grandfather take care of her.

"Holly, Megan, and I love to hear Megan's step mom, Julie, and Dr. Clery talk about it. He says stuff like, 'The men in my church and your dads counseled me against taking on a woman's role. But I said, I guess God gave me a father's role when he gave me my little Meg, and that means doing what's best for her. The wee one had already lost her mother, and I was the closest one to her. I knew her needs, and I loved meeting them. Besides, the last words my dear wife said to me were, "Colin, I'm quite ready to go home to Jesus because I know you'll take loving care of our little Meg." But I'll tell you the truth, it was Meg that took care of me. Without my little Meg to love on, I don't think I could have gone on living.

"'I told Rob and Vern that I didn't see the word "role" in the Bible at all, but I saw "love" plenty. I told them that I didn't think those two words got on well together. "Role" seemed like playing a part because you are a certain brand of person. It's thinking you know what to do before you really know what a person needs. "Love" listens to the person in front of me and responds according to what it hears, both from that person and from God. It relates to a particular person in particular circumstances, and I've seen quite a wide variety of circumstances. I was sure my responsibility was to do what was best for wee Meg. I knew her best and loved her best; therefore, I should take care of her.' Holly and I love our dads, and we have

Chapter 15

always known that they loved us. But Dr. Clery and Megan have something really special; their relationship is direct; it's unmediated through roles. When Megan was in junior high, she started doing some dumb stuff. Dr. Clery just told her to stop, and she did. He wasn't acting out his role as her father; he was just loving her. She wasn't acting out her role as an obedient daughter; she was responding to his love. God's love is the source of their relationship, and they are both tapped into it. That's the kind of relationships Holly and I want."

Nora said, "It does indeed sound like a beautiful relationship. On our good days, it's how my husband and I relate. I have always been thankful that he was more interested in loving than in role playing. I wonder if that attitude of Dr. Clery's wasn't part of his success as a principal? If the teachers felt the presence of real servant leadership, they likely appreciated him."

Jill said, "Yeah, he was really popular with the teachers, even though Julie says he made them work harder than the other principal."

Jill continued, "Dr. Clery says that 'roles' are temporary and ought to be held according to gifts. He says that as a P.E. teacher, his role was to get the freshman boys fit. As the principal his role was to lead the school. The school needed both jobs done. He says that a good principal understands the knowledge, experience, and personalities of his or her staff and matches the person to the role no matter what that person's permanent class—like race or gender. To say a man must be the freshman P.E. teacher forever because he's black only announces the principal's racism. To say a woman can never be a priest no matter what her spiritual gifts only announces the Church's sexism. Black men with the gift of administration should be principals, and women with gifts of spiritual leadership should be priests. I have known many in both classes. Roles are temporary, indeed; I think all good principals should have previously been good teachers. Megan's mom and dad frequently say stuff like that."

Nora replied, "It sounds like Megan has a good relationship with her stepmother."

"She really does," agreed Jill. "Julie was a very close friend of Megan's real mom. They both worked at St. James. She even helped take care of Megan when her mom was sick and her dad was still working. It was after Julie watched Dr. Clery taking such great care of Megan for several years that she grew into loving him in a different way than just friendship. Dr. Clery teases Megan by saying that she got a wife for him when she was only five years old. Julie also really respected Dr. Clery for being so comfortable taking directions from and being so supportive of the new principal. When the other principal retired, the school board offered him back his old job. He is again the favorite principal."

"I can understand why you think so highly of the Clery family," said Nora. "It appears they model a kind of relationship that you deeply desire . . . That is perhaps different from what you knew during your childhood?"

"It wasn't until I was in high school that I considered that my dad might not be the best dad in the world. He took good care of us. He always went to my swim and track meets. He read to us. Most of the time he treated my mom really well. But I just don't want their kind of relationship . . ."

Nora said nothing, just continued with her brew for a few moments until Jill continued.

"Last year my mom was driving us home from school, and our white Suburban broke down. It wasn't a big deal. My mom cell-phoned a tow truck, which took our car and us to our mechanic's shop. My dad picked us up there. And on the way home he said, 'Juanita, I think it's time you get a new car.'

"My Mom said, 'I'd like to wait until after I've paid for new latrines at the orphanage. I've committed to that, and I don't think I can do both on my allowance.'

"My dad just said, 'I'd like you to get the new car first.' I felt like screaming at him. I knew my mom would just get the new car. They wouldn't argue; she'd just been trumped . . . My mom had been so excited about new latrines for an orphanage in Kenya where she had gone on a short-term mission trip. The mechanic had said that the Suburban didn't need a major repair, and that he could easily make it dependable again. I thought, and maybe I was wrong, that my dad was really concerned about my mom driving around in an older car, weakening his image as our provider.

"I want to decide things together if I ever get married. I want the same kind of voice as my husband. I don't want to stubbornly insist on my own way; real submission is beautiful. But I want my own voice. I know it may be more difficult in some ways, but I want to agree with my husband. I want to do and to decide together. I never had to deal with quarreling at home because my mom thinks she's supposed to follow my dad's leadership. I would have loved to hear them argue, respectfully of course. If only I could have heard my mom really try to persuade my dad of something, I would have been much happier. When I think or feel strongly about something,

Chapter 15

I want to say so. Holly feels the same way as I do, even though her parents bickered a lot at home."

"Are you saying they did not bicker elsewhere?" asked Nora.

"Holly's dad is an OB/GYN, and her mom is a nurse-midwife. They work together beautifully in the same hospital. Dr. Billingham is always bragging about how great Clare is at helping mothers during labor. When Mrs. Billingham first graduated from nursing school, she worked at a very primitive, mission hospital in Guatemala. Dr. Billingham says she learned how to really see and hear a laboring mother without an overdependence on machines. Yet she knows how to appreciate their appropriate use. He says he can really depend on her to accurately assess how a labor is progressing and make sure a mother gets the care she needs.

"One weekend when I was little and my parents were out of town, I was staying with Holly's family when there was an emergency at the hospital. Holly, Darren, and I had to hang out in the doctor's lounge because no babysitter was available. Seeing them work together in a crisis and discuss treatment was one of the most beautiful things I've ever seen. They were just so much on the same wavelength. They understood each other so well and worked together like clockwork.

"At home they're always bickering. Mrs. Billingham says, 'A hospital must have a hierarchy. It's right that the surgeon has the last word. He has a responsibility that a nurse does not have. I respect that. But a home should not be like a hospital. A mother and a father share responsibility for their children. A mother has insights a father needs to hear, and the running of the home is just as much on her shoulders. The hierarchy thing doesn't belong in the home.' But Dr. Billingham expects to be the boss at home too. She resents that, and he's threatened by that resentment. Sometimes I was uncomfortable staying there because of the tension.

"I love Holly's parents, but I can understand why she wants a different kind of marriage. Sometimes I think Holly loves maternity wards so much because that's where she has seen her parents loving each other so well. When that aspect of their life together is brought home, peace reigns. Fetal stress and maternal hemorrhage are frequent subjects of dinner conversation at the Billingham's, and everybody's interested. Darren, my future brother-in-law, wants to be an OB/GYN, but he's really glad my sister, Katie, studies architecture. He says that when they are married, they will have many subjects to talk peacefully about. Darren and Katie think about marriage like Holly and I, and we've talked about it a lot. It will be so fun to visit them after they're married."

"So," responded Nora, "you want a marriage based on mutuality, not hierarchy, so it makes you afraid to go to church?"

"The Sunday after the Suburban broke down, our pastor preached on Ephesians 5:22–24 in a way that made my dad feel justified for telling my mom to get a new car. After church my mom called the orphanage director in tears and didn't feel like eating for two days. On Monday she went to the car dealership and bought a new white Suburban and was grouchy the rest of the week. That's also when she started being critical of our pastor. I don't think my mom or Holly's mom really trust him that much anymore. But our dads really like him. Our dads are both deacons; our moms just complain about him to each other when they think we can't hear."

Chapter 16

It does not profit a man to marry. For what is a woman but an enemy of friendship, an inescapable punishment, a necessary evil, a natural temptation, a domestic danger, delectable mischief, a fault in nature, painted with beautiful colors? . . . The whole of her body is nothing less than phlegm, blood, bile, rheum and the fluid of digested food . . . If you consider what is stored up behind those lovely eyes, the angle of the nose, the mouth and the cheeks you will agree that the well-proportioned body is only a whitened sepulchre.

—St. John Chrysostom

How great is the devotion of this woman, that she would be even counted worthy of the appellation of apostle.

—St. John Chrysostom, speaking of Junia in Romans 16:7[1]

On Thursday evening at seven-thirty Ted Mullins pulled his ski cap down over his ears as he headed back to campus. He had borrowed his mother's car for the day, so he could stay late for the large-group IV meeting. Uncle Hank left campus at five o'clock, and IV didn't begin until eight o'clock. He had come in early this morning and parked in the structure next to the library. His last class ended at two o'clock; after which he had spent a productive four hours researching for his philosophy paper. He had decided to write that paper on the influence of Greek gender philosophy on the church fathers, and unfortunately his argument had been easy to research. How could such smart guys have such an incredible blind spot? It baffled him.

In the morning Dr. Shaw had passed back the paper he wrote on Roger Nicole's interpretation of Genesis 2. She always listed grade results on the

---

1. In Schaff and Wace, *Select Library of Nicene and Post-Nicene Fathers I*, 11:555.

board. She put the highest score on top and all the other scores in descending order. Next to the score she wrote the number of students who earned that grade. The practice did not promote competition, and yet it gave students a way of realistically assessing the quality of their scholarship. At the top of the list was "98 percent" and next to it a 3. Dr. Shaw always handed back their work upside down, so she didn't advertise people's grades. But Dana Blevin sat in front of Ted, and he couldn't help but notice that Dana's paper, on some fragments of Sappho's poetry, earned a 98 percent. Ted wasn't surprised; Dana seemed so sensitive to poetic language. And he was patient and could tease out the meaning. He guessed the other 98 percent belonged to Travis Williams who had written an excellent paper on Hesiod.

Ted had really taken his topic for that paper on a dare from Dr. Shaw. His working thesis had been, "Roger Nicole makes several errors in his purely egalitarian interpretation of Genesis 2." But Ted found he could not deconstruct Nicole's argument on any point. His final thesis had read, "In spite of almost complete denial by contemporary American Evangelicals, Roger Nicole accurately and consistently explicates Genesis 2." His conclusion had surprised himself. Every family on Mullins Mountain maintained some variation on the "men are the leaders of the family" theme, and all of them were strong, loving families. But after writing his paper, he had been noticing that the men on the mountain seldom took any sort of leadership that was essentially different than their wives. They had all married women whose faith and intellectual development they respected. All of them listened carefully to what their wives said, and he could not remember a time when one of them had made a major decision without the agreement of his wife. They said they believed in male leadership, but Ted was beginning to think that in practice it was actually mutual submission.

After the four hours of research in the afternoon, he had been happy to get out in the cold and keep his date at Wild Mushroom with his cousin, Lydia. She was one of the eight Michael Mullinses. Ted was one of the nine James Mullinses. Uncle Hank and Aunt Kathy only had only three children, a very small family for Mullins Mountain. Ted and Lydia both loved a specialty pizza at Wild Mushroom called Philosopher's Pie, a Greek pizza with kalamata olives, mushrooms, thinly sliced steak, marinated artichoke hearts, feta, and most importantly, a generous dose of fresh garlic. If they each paid half, they felt justified in ordering a large.

Lydia was only two months younger than he, so it was likely she wouldn't be home much longer either. She hoped to study classics, and was

Chapter 16

gifted in both Latin and Greek. They both loved zip lines, and together they had installed three great lines on the mountain for their siblings and cousins, not to mention themselves. He and Lydia had something special; somehow they were just on the same wavelength. If he went away to school next year, he would miss her terribly.

At the end of Howard Street he decided to walk through the parking structure hoping to avoid some of that cold wind. Why was he always so excited about IV? He really liked Shane, the director. He also liked the worship music. But he suspected it might be because of his interest in that tall, fawn-like girl that always came with Doug's friend, Holly. Ted met Doug, who was from Charlotte, in his philosophy class.

The mysterious fawn-like girl had large, liquid, dark brown eyes, and she seemed so . . . shy? No, not shy—something else. He did not know what. He had wanted to meet her for several weeks, but still didn't even know her name. A couple meetings ago he had watched her from the other side of the room as Holly and Doug were chatting. She had not entered the conversation at all. There was something illusive about her. Last week he had offered her a cup of tea at the refreshment table, but this week, if she came, he would really try to introduce himself. She'd be obliged at least to tell him her name.

Back out into that darn wind as he exited the parking structure, he wished the bookstore was still open. That was the student union's closest door to him now. But he braved the wind the length of the solarium and entered the warm building. He climbed the stairs to the second floor, detecting the aroma of burritos under construction in the Cascade Cafe. Usually that scent made his stomach growl, but tonight that organ was full of exactly one half of a large Philosopher's Pie. He and his satiated appetite marched down the hall and entered the Lindville Falls room, reserved by IV.

About fifty students were already standing around in small groups. Ted suspected the dialogs ranged from idle chatter and gossip to serious academic and personal conversations. IV friendships developed quickly among people who attended the same small-group Bible study. On the far side of the room a group of four, that included Doug and Holly, were chatting merrily. Disappointed, he noticed that "Fawn-girl" was not among them.

Miriam and Tran walked to the front and began tuning their guitars. Gary sat down to his pair of congas. Shane finished shaking hands with a first-time visitor and sat down in the front row. People began taking their seats. Ted saw Holly look around for somebody; then she chose a chair, one from the aisle, obviously saving it for somebody.

They began with one of Ted's favorite invocational hymns, "Come, Thou Almighty King." He loved the rich, old lyrics combined with the lively guitars and beat of the drums. The IV folks were enthusiastic worshippers; he felt among like-minded friends. By the time they had gotten to "Come, and Thy people bless, And give Thy word success," the fawn-girl had taken the saved seat next to Holly.

As Ted again admired her beauty, he was suddenly startled by a tiny, but protrusive lump in the front of her waist. This was a particularly fit young woman. She would not be putting on a little extra weight in quite that shape. He realized immediately that she was pregnant and that he was disconcerted by her pregnancy. Questions flooded in. Was she married? Was she loose? He didn't even know her. It was such an insignificant little lump; would anybody else even notice? Why did he care so much? If she was married, why didn't she come to IV with her husband? If she was loose, why would she want to come to IV at all?

He suddenly recalled an admonition his grandmother sometimes gave. "If you find your neighbor's sin suddenly more interesting than your own, then it's time for confession of your own." Out of the corner of his eye, he watched her worship. He felt that she meant the words she was singing. "Spirit of holiness, On us descend." He sang those same words and also meant them. But he was so ruffled that he couldn't concentrate on Shane's sermon.

Ted was aware that Shane was emphasizing the revolutionary and anti-cultural way that Jesus treated women. Ted was cognizant that at one point Shane read Luke 10:38–42 and then asked, "Martha played a woman's role, and Mary listened to Jesus. Which did Jesus think was better? Can you do both?"

Ted wished he could concentrate because what did make its way into his brain was important and profound. But he could only focus on that beautiful, pregnant girl, not fifteen feet away from him, who was not wearing a wedding ring. And the questions kept firing. By the time Shane had finished his sermon, Ted had come to a few conclusions. He had decided that what he had been tempted to call shyness had been both embarrassment about her condition and fear of guys. For he had seen her meet women and converse comfortably with them. It was only guys from whom she seemed to need to protect herself. She blocked Doug out as completely

Chapter 16

as if he wasn't there at all. Ted also concluded that she wasn't loose. For if she was embarrassed about being pregnant and loose, she probably would have had an abortion. What he couldn't understand at all was his own intense interest—It was absolutely none of his business. And yet he was more determined than ever to meet her.

He suddenly became aware that he was singing "Blessed Be Your Name" with the others and that it was the right thing for her and him to be singing. So he sang it with all his heart. Then Shane closed with a quotation.

> Perhaps it is no wonder that women were the first at the Cradle and the last at the Cross. They had never known a man like this Man—there never has been another. A prophet and teacher who never nagged at them, never flattered or coaxed or patronized; who never made arch jokes about them, never treated them as "the women, God help us" or "the ladies, God bless them!"; who rebuked without querulousness and praised without condescension; who took their arguments seriously; who never mapped out their sphere for them, never urged them to be feminine or jeered at them for being female; who had no axe to grind and no uneasy male dignity to defend; who took them as he found them and was completely unself-conscious. There is no act, no sermon, no parable in the whole Gospel that borrows its pungency from female perversity; nobody could possibly guess from the words or deeds of Jesus that there was anything "funny" about woman's nature.[2]

Then Shane said, "Thanks for coming; now go in peace to love and serve the Lord."

The students rose as a body, reached for backpacks and jackets, and said their goodbyes. For it was nine o'clock, and most of them still had a few hours of homework. But Ted did not hesitate. He was convinced the fawn-girl was someone exceptional, and he wanted to know her and her story. Holly conferred with Doug while the fawn-girl was standing back and ignoring him. Ted advanced between them, feeling temporarily bold. He said, "Hi, I've seen you here several times this semester. My name is Theodore Mullins, but only my mother calls me that when she's mad at me. The rest of the time I'm Ted." And he extended his right hand.

She moved slowly but deliberately in response. She looked him in the face with tears in rivulets trickling down her cheeks and managed to say, "Hi, I'm Jill Kelley."

---

2. Sayers, *Are Women Human?*, 47.

Ted pretended not to notice the tears, but responded to the smile with one of his own. "I got lucky in the library this afternoon, so I'm calling it a day. I hope you don't still have stacks of homework tonight?"

The tears flowed even more freely as she took a deep breath and sighed rather than spoke. "I'll just put the finishing touches on a color project for my design class." Ted sensed that the sentence caused a major release of tension. Although she was crying, he felt it had somehow been good for her to talk to him.

Holly, Miriam, and Doug turned toward them, and Holly said, "We're going to stop at the Cascades and get a hot chocolate before heading back to the dorm. Want to join us?"

Ted said, "Sounds good." Jill nodded. Ted noticed that she couldn't talk once Doug had joined the conversation. The five of them walked downstairs and over to the hot drink machine in the café. They each filled a sixteen-ounce paper cup with steamed milk and then stirred in a scoop of cocoa powder. The others swiped their BlueridgeCards for the cashier, and Ted handed her a dollar and two quarters. Since he lived off campus, he didn't put money in a meal account.

Usually on school days he just brought a peanut butter and honey sandwich. But he considered it a gourmet delight. His mother's homemade whole wheat bread was fresh and fantastic. He ground the peanut butter himself at Earth Food. Even the honey was special, from hives on Mullins Mountain cared for by his cousin, Andy, who was really into bees. He had only eaten in a dining commons a few times.

The round lounge area just outside the Cascade offered a quantity of round stainless steel tables with four matching stainless steel chairs. Doug grabbed a chair from the next table and made a cozy place for five. Ted asked Doug and Holly, "How did you guys meet? Seems like you knew each other before coming to Blue Ridge."

Doug answered, "Holly and I both went to Concord High School, and we were both in the Medical Explorers Club on campus. So we hung out together some the last two years of high school. Miriam also went to Concord, but we didn't meet her until IV."

Holly added, "But the last I had heard during spring of our senior year, Doug was going to UNC Charlotte. I was really surprised when I ran into him in the library right before school started."

Doug said, "It was all very last minute. My dad's company transferred him to Asheville, so my parents decided to sell the house. I had applied and

Chapter 16

been accepted at Blue Ridge, but I originally decided on UNC Charlotte so I could live at home to save money. Without that option, Blue Ridge was my first choice."

Ted turned to Jill, "But how did you meet Holly?"

Jill looked up and smiled, but no words came.

After an awkward pause, Holly answered for her. "Oh, Jill and I have been friends forever. We were neighbors and even went to the same church in Concord. Even our parents are good friends. But Jill went to a private high school called Covenant Classical School, so she never met Doug until Blue Ridge. We came here with another good friend from our neighborhood called Megan. She doesn't come to IV, but goes to CCM. We're all roommates in Gorman."

Miriam joined in with, "Doug and I both live in Hodge Hall. Where do you live, Ted?"

Ted replied, "I'm probably just at Blue Ridge for a year while I figure out a good school for theology. I live with my family on a sort of family compound just outside Cross Valley. My grandparents bought the mountain a long time ago when it was cheap. When my father and each of his three brothers married, they received about thirty-five acres as a wedding present. So that about covers Mullins Mountain. The place is crawling with cousins. I ride in to campus with my Uncle Hank; he is a computer science professor here."

Then Jill surprised them all by looking straight at Ted and saying, "That sounds delightful." Now Ted saw that Holly was teary, and Doug sat open mouthed.

Ted just grinned and said, "It is most of the time; at least there's never a dull moment."

Doug asked, "Hey, Miriam, have you finished your essay for freshman comp? I'll edit yours if you'll edit mine."

Miriam answered, "Yea, I've got a draft done, but it needs a second pair of eyes. Isn't yours due in the morning? We'd better get to it before I crash."

Holly interjected, "Oh shoot, I've still got anatomy to memorize. Are you ready to go, Jill?" Jill didn't answer, but stood and hauled her backpack to her shoulders.

Ted said, "If I don't get my mom's car back home by ten, I won't get it again for a long time. I guess this party's over. See you guys." They all threw their cups into the recycling container marked "Paper" and went in three directions, Doug and Miriam toward Hodge, Holly and Jill toward Gorman, and Ted toward the library parking structure.

As Ted hoofed along in front of the Solarium, he could see Jill and Holly across Avery Mall bowing into the wind, huddling together arm-in-arm for mutual protection from the cold. Aiming for the tunnel under River Street, they looked so vulnerable. It suddenly occurred to him what a joy it would be to help ease their way. He liked Holly. But thinking of his relationship to that beautiful Jill across the common, he was reminded of a day last winter when he, with his father's pickup, had hauled Lydia's Toyota up out of the little canyon next to the lane on the mountain.

Rain had fallen in the night, and then the temperature had suddenly dropped very low. The ice was thick but invisible. Lydia had very carefully eased out of her driveway to head down the lane. She had a tutorial in Charlotte on Wednesday mornings. But as soon as the lane began its steep decline, she lost all control. The Toyota turned perpendicular to the lane, bolted to the canyon bottom, and came to a sudden halt. Lydia and her car were unscathed, ready to move, but utterly without traction. She could no more have driven up the canyon wall than his grandmother could have denied Christ. She had trudged up to his house and rapped on his and Sam's bedroom window. When he lifted the window, Lydia had said, "Oh Ted, I don't want to be late for my Greek lesson. I landed in the canyon bottom. Please help me."

He put on his shoes and jacket then went to the garage. He said, "Hop in my dad's pickup," as he lifted the keys from their hook on the wall. He grabbed some adjustable chains from a shelf under the workbench, dropped them in the truck bed, and joined Lydia in the cab. The one-ton truck was four-wheel-drive with winter tires and a winch. He drove the few hundred yards down the lane and parked sideways on the pavement just above Lydia's Toyota. He remembered setting the parking brake and blocking the wheels as he had been taught. He went to the nose, disengaged the spool on the winch, and scooted into the canyon holding the hook. The cable unwound obediently behind him. He looped the cable through the Toyota's chassis front, and then climbed back up to the lane. He and Lydia had just stood there watching after the winch began slowly winding itself back up. First the winch dragged the front of the Toyota around so that the two vehicles were headlight to headlight. The powerful motor turned its tiny gear, and Lydia's car crept up the icy canyon's side.

Chapter 16

That's what was happening now. He was standing on the high, firm road watching as a powerful force gradually drew the one who had been stuck up to him. He could do nothing to help but access another power source. So he prayed, "Dear Father, I feel your power drawing this Jill to yourself and to me. Please give me all I need to help her on her way. Please put her back on a firm path, unharmed. Amen."

When Lydia's Toyota had reached the roadside, he had stopped the winch, put chains on its two front tires, then unhooked the cable from the car. Lydia got behind her steering wheel with a huge and appreciative smile. He plopped in the passenger seat, and rode down the hill with her. At the highway he got out and took off the chains. He remembered standing at the edge of the highway with the chains dangling from his left fist and happily waving Lydia off with his right.

Hiking back up the hill he had felt a deep satisfaction that Lydia would get to Greek on time . . . No, that wasn't it. It was for himself. He had been used to help someone he loved. All the power to help had come from his Dad's truck. If Uncle Michael had a truck like his Dad's and had taught Lydia to use it, he had done nothing she could not have done for herself. He had done nothing but make himself available to serve. God provided everything else. It seemed so simple, but it was true. Joy comes from loving and trusting God and serving others. That evening Lydia had shown up with a flourless chocolate torte—his absolute favorite. But that feeling of joy he had had that morning in the lane beat even flourless chocolate torte.

Ted sensed Jill needed his help; at the same time he realized that he had no idea how to help. As Holly and Jill disappeared from sight, Ted prayed, "I trust You for all resources and wisdom; please let me help Jill."

As Ted tried to slip in quietly through the kitchen door, he heard his Mom say, "Just in the nick of time—How did your day go?" She spoke from the quilting frame she was working over.

"Fine," he said as he grabbed a meatball out of the left-over spaghetti sauce she was allowing to cool before covering to refrigerate.

"I'd prefer a bit more detail. How about a blow by blow?" she asked.

As soon as the chewed meatball was descending his esophagus, Ted said, "I'm not sure you'll be comfortable with one of the details. I can truthfully say that I'm fine; why don't you sleep on that?"

"You've stirred up my curiosity now; I can handle an uncomfortable detail, especially since you are still fine. I'm hanging in there for the blow-by-blow," was her retort.

"You asked for it. Don't say I didn't warn you . . . Dr. Shaw handed back our essays this morning, and two others and I got 98 percents," he began.

"Congratulations, but I don't think that is likely to make me too uncomfortable," she replied with a proud grin.

The next blow was, "I finished my research for my philosophy paper this afternoon. For being incredibly smart guys, the church fathers are downright prejudiced when it comes to women. They swallowed Greek misogyny hook, line, and sinker."

"I'm sorry to hear it, but at least you'll have an easy time writing your paper," replied Magdalene Mullins.

"I met Lydia at Wild Mushroom for dinner, and we split a large Philosopher's Pie half 'n half, both the bill and the pizza," Ted stated.

"That sounds perfectly equitable, and explains why you only stole one leftover meatball. I waited to put them in the fridge till you got home, thinking you might be ravenous."

"Where's Dad?" asked Ted.

"He needs to catch an early flight out of Charlotte in the morning, so he went to bed after tucking Sammy and Bret in . . . Isn't there a missing detail?"

"Well there's an interesting girl in IV that I've been wanting to meet. Tonight I did, and I think she's pregnant."

His mother's humor evaporated like a snowflake in a hot skillet. "Oh, Theo," she breathed with concern and laid down her needle and thread. "Is she married?" Her son had never had a girlfriend, and she had not imagined his first interest would be in a pregnant woman.

"She's a freshman living in a dorm—I doubt if she's married . . . I warned you that it might not sit well. In spite of the pregnant part, I sense she's a mature believer with some sort of trouble I can help her with. Why I think that, I haven't the faintest idea—only I prayed for guidance about her, and I think I got it. The only thing I know for sure about her is that she is the prettiest girl on campus. I am also praying that if I'm supposed to befriend her, an opportunity will appear on a silver platter. You might be tempted to pray that I'll never see her again, but I'd rather you didn't . . . Maybe you could pray that if we would not be good friends for each other, He would make it clear to me?"

"I guess that sounds fair enough, but, Theo, please be very careful," she pleaded.

"I promise I will. What time will Dad leave the house in the morning?"

Chapter 16

She answered, "He says he must be out the door by six."

"Good, I'll stumble out at five-thirty and have coffee with him. I want to tell him about Jill myself. OK?"

"I'm sure he'd appreciate you talking to him about Jill," his mother replied.

"Yeah, I thought so too. Where's he going?"

"Western Kenya. There's been horrible flooding in the lower Yala River Basin. He's doing a 'needs assessment' for SR."

"Isn't that in the Nyanza Province, northwest of Kisumu?" asked Ted. The son of an international disaster relief assessor knows African geography. Ted and Sammy had a huge world map on the wall of their room, and Ted used it to teach his six-year-old brother geography. They had a box of red pushpins, and they put one in at every one of their father's work sites. They had them sticking in every continent, but Africa looked like a large version of their mother's pin cushion. It was a very needy continent. Ted wished his father was home more, but he was deeply proud of the work he did. James Mullins served the poorest of the poor when they needed it most, and he could not imagine more satisfying work.

He had already passed down the joy of service to his elder children. Ted's oldest brother, Jared, had earned a master's in international development at Fuller and worked in the projects department at Saints' Resources. He and his wife Mary lived in Poplar with their little son, Tommy. Ted and Sammy already had a good sprinkling of blue pushpins which meant Jared. His oldest sister, Zoe, was finishing up law school while doing an internship with IJM. She wanted to advocate for women who had been sold into the sex trade. She was represented by a single green pushpin in Calcutta. He was very proud of his brother and sister, but Ted was becoming convinced that he belonged among long relationships with people in a church and books in a library.

"I better hit the hay if I'm going to have coffee with Dad. Uncle Hank's picking me up at seven-thirty tomorrow. G' night, Mom," he said as he kissed her cheek. "And please don't worry."

"Worry is indeed an unprofitable activity, but it's an occupational hazard for mothers of nine. It will help me not to worry, Theo, if you keep me updated about your relationship with Jill."

"I promise."

"Good night, my son. I appreciate your openness."

Chapter 17

A wife of noble character who can find?
She is worth far more than rubies.
Her husband has full confidence in her
and lacks nothing of value.

—PROVERBS 31:10–11

ON NOVEMBER 5 NORA arrived at Expresso Yosef at a quarter to four. She was glad to get there before Jill. She needed a few moments to sit quietly and transition from the traffic jam that had been office hours. Her announcement that no make-up quizzes would be given after Thanksgiving had stirred the procrastinators into action. Most students in 2030 were now working on their final essay. Nora ran office hours as first come, first served, which was best most of the time, but not today. At one point in the afternoon she had two students in the faculty lounge taking quizzes and one sitting on the floor in the hall with a clipboard while she made suggestions for revision to a paper in her office. She thought, "Oh well, at least everybody was seen—if not given the usual personal attention."

After half and half had been added to her Kenyan decaf, she climbed the stairs to the cozy corner to wait for Jill. Nora made mental notes of some subjects she meant to discuss with Jill. According to the mentor outline she was supposed to discuss fetal development and maternal nutrition. This seemed important not only for the relevant content, but because Promise had an incentive program by which Jill could earn baby furniture for completing all topics on the mentor syllabus. Nora prioritized other topics to bring up. Running excessively, talking to young men, studying successfully, and attending church seemed important matters. As Nora was praying a blessing on Jill and their meeting, she heard a sprightly step ascending the stairs. Nora was surprised when Jill's smiling countenance rose above floor

Chapter 17

level in the stairwell. Didn't Jill know she was an abused victim and ought to be depressed?

She clearly was not at all despondent, but smiling eagerly. Nora put her plan on the back burner, for Jill obviously had another story to tell.

Nora said, "Great to see you looking so well. May I get you a cup of coffee?"

Jill answered, "Hi. No thanks, I don't want the baby having caffeine, and I'm still developing a taste for decaf." Jill reached in her backpack and pulled out a beautiful Fuji apple. "I've got something yummy. Privette gets great local, organic apples." Nora noted there was no need for a crash course on maternal nutrition.

Nora began with, "If I was going to guess, I'd say something good happened recently. I'd love a good story."

"Good guess," commented Jill. "I can't wait to tell you some things."

"I'm all ears," said Nora. And she was.

"Do you remember me telling you about the guy who gave me a cup of tea at IV?" Nora nodded. "Well, I met him, and I talked to him. I even went to his house and met his family."

"How did that happen?" asked Nora.

"Well after the IV meeting, he just came up and introduced himself. I told him my name. It was really hard, but I forced myself. Holly asked him to join Doug, Miriam, she and I for hot chocolate, and he did. I really liked him, and he told a little about his family. It made me want to meet them.

"Well the next day, which was Friday, I was thinking about how interesting he was. It made me think of Cascades because that was where we had the hot chocolate. So after my math class I decided to go to Cascades for lunch and get their beans and rice. And there he was, sitting at the same table where we had gone after IV! I plucked up my courage and walked over to him and said, 'Hi.'

"I could tell he was really surprised. He stood up to greet me, and then asked me to have a seat. When I sat down, he pulled out a package wrapped in butcher paper and said, 'I make a terrific peanut butter sandwich, how about half?'

"I said, 'I'll eat half of your sandwich if you'll eat some of the beans and rice plate I am planning to get.' And I felt like talking; I wasn't forcing myself. I felt sort of normal again."

Nora interjected, "Wonderful."

Jill went on. "It really was delicious. Huge, thick slices of fresh, homemade, whole-wheat bread slathered with fresh-ground peanut butter and luscious honey. I don't usually think of a peanut butter sandwich as anything to rave about, but it was great. Then I went and got my beans and rice with an extra plate. It felt so good to share with him.

"He told me about harvesting the honey that had been on the sandwich with his cousin. Then he asked me about how my classes were going.

"I told him they were OK, except that I needed some carefully chosen scraps of fabric for my textile project. I told him I had gone out the 421 on the AppalCart that morning to the only fabric store in Poplar to see if they had any scraps for giveaway. But I think every design major at Blue Ridge had been there asking for scraps. They said that they have a half yard minimum purchase. I need about six different fabrics to put on my foam core display, but I only need four inch squares. I told him that my mom had a big basket of fabric scraps and remnants, but I didn't know how I could get to Concord. To buy all that fabric would be such a waste, and it would use up my allowance for the rest of the semester. I told him I was having trouble deciding what to do."

Nora wondered where this was leading, but not for long.

Jill continued, "I couldn't believe it when he said, 'Maybe I can help. Are you busy this evening?' I said I was just planning to worry about how I was going to get my textile project done. Then he pulled out his phone, and called his mom.

"I could hear her answer, 'Hi, Theo, What's up?'

"He said, 'Hey Mom, you know that big basket where you toss all your bits and pieces of leftover fabric—Can I bring a friend over this evening to rummage through it, and maybe take some pieces? And can she come for dinner?'

"I heard her say, 'Certainly, I don't hoard my fabric scraps. She's welcome to join us for dinner, but warn her that it will be very simple. I told Jared and Mary that I'd watch Tommy for them tonight. Lillian's planning on just making a big pot of stuff from the garden, but I'm sure there'll be plenty.'

"Ted said, 'Great, we'll see you later. Thanks, Mom. Bye.'

"Then he said to me, 'It may not be anything special for dinner, but if you're pleased with a peanut butter sandwich, maybe you'll be alright with Lillian's "pot of something?"

Chapter 17

"I just said, 'Sure, home-cooked whatever sounds better than Privette anything. Thanks very much.'"

Nora tried to ask almost without interest, "Did you say his name is Ted?"

"Yeah, his name is Ted Mullins," said Jill without stopping for a breath. "Then he said, 'I've gotta go to my philosophy class. Can you meet me at five o'clock at the Raley AppalCart stop? My Uncle Hank picks me up there. I can bring you back this evening whenever you're ready.' I just said, 'Thanks a lot. I'll be there—like I talk to guys all the time.'"

Nora shoved her recognition of Ted under the rug of confidentiality, and delightedly commented, "That is excellent progress. This young man certainly has a gift for putting you at ease. How did your visit go?"

"It was really good. He has a huge family, and everybody was welcoming. And there was so much going on that I didn't have to be a center of attention. Ted was always nearby and very aware of me, and I could tell his mom wanted to get to know me. But she had her hands full with her little grandson and all the others.

"She had a humungous stash of scraps and remnants. She does quilting and upholstery, so there was a vast choice of fabrics. His mom has excellent taste in color and texture. I found a perfect tapestry for the sofa in my project and all the other fabrics I needed.

"Dinner was so fun. Ted's fourteen-year-old sister, Lillian, made a huge tureen of Italian butternut squash stew. It contained delicious homemade sausage and home-dried herbs from her garden. Lily, that's what Ted calls her, just put a stack of bowls, spoons, and the tureen at the end of the long trestle table in front of Mrs. Mullins. She prayed, and dished all ten of us up.

"There was more of the great bread I had tasted at lunch in the middle of the table. I didn't sit by Ted because his little nephew, Tommy, who was in a high-chair next to Mrs. Mullins, insisted that his 'Unca Te,' sit beside him. He's two, and he can't pronounce 'uncle' yet nor remember the 'D.'

"Everybody talked and enjoyed themselves, but there was only one conversation. Usually when there's so many people at a table, there are several conversations going. But nobody interrupted, not even six-year-old Sammy. Bret (she's eight) asked me about my family, and Allison was very interested in my textile project. Mrs. Mullins told about Mr. Mullins almost missing a quick connection to Nairobi at Heathrow, and that they should hear by the morning that he is in Nyanza Province. Twleve-year-old Kaj told about how the chickens have almost stopped laying because of the cold. Walker and his cousin Forrest, who are in high-school but taking classes at Caldwell Community College, talked about an interesting lecture that they had heard in their Spanish class about the syncretism of Catholicism and tribal religions in southern Mexico. Sammy showed everybody a thorn cut he had received on his arm. He also insisted on reading aloud a few pages from *One Fish, Two Fish, Red Fish, Blue Fish* to prove to the whole family that he could read. Ten-year-old Allison asked if the Peter Mullinses were coming down for Thanksgiving, and was disappointed to hear that she would not be seeing her cousin Jenny until Christmas. It was an energetic, respectful hodgepodge of a conversation. I loved it.

"After dinner their cousin August, who plays the piano beautifully, came over to practice some songs that Lillian, Kaj, and Walker would play with him at Poplar Bible Fellowship on Sunday. Lillian plays the violin, Walker the viola, and Kaj the drums. They asked Ted and I to critique their new arrangement. Mrs. Mullins sang; little Tommy danced, and Sammy played with Legos in the corner of the room. It was a really fun evening."

"Ted certainly seems blessed with a rich family life," enthused Nora. "Is he involved at PBF?"

Jill looked curiously at Nora and said, "It's funny you should ask that because that's what we talked about while he was driving me home. Ted grew up in that church, and he has many great friends there. He still goes there on Sundays, but he's not comfortable with their doctrine about women. He alluded to some sort of recent scandal there. Ted thinks they are handling it well, but he wonders if that sort of thing would happen so often in churches if women had a different kind of voice in the church. He told me that he thinks he may be called to the ministry, and that he's been struggling with what the Bible says concerning women. He's also been studying the history of doctrines about women, and he doesn't want to be part of perpetuating error. Ted told me that at this point in his understanding, if he was a church leader, he could not exclude women from leadership in the church or family because he doesn't think that is what the Bible teaches. When he said that, I was just hoping he was right because I've been praying for forgiveness for thinking the Bible had some ugly parts. The hope that it might just be my pastor in Concord's interpretation that was ugly made me feel so light.

"Ted also said that Shane asked him to help do some IV large-group teaching about it. I told him that Shane is very careful about the

Chapter 17

quality of the teaching at IV, so he should really consider it an honor that he was asked."

"It seems providential that you two should become friends just when you are both working through the same issues," replied Nora.

Jill said, "It really does, and I told him that Holly and I weren't going to church until we could find one with both a high view of Scripture and a strong women's voice. I feel like I can trust Ted like I had thought never to be able to trust again. I think God put him in my life."

Nora agreed, "I'm sure He has."

Jill went on, "And I've been considering the possibility of telling Ted about the frat party and my pregnancy." This statement led to a prolonged pause in the conversation.

Finally Nora said, "Yours is the sort of story that will make you very vulnerable. If Ted stays fully in your friendship after you tell him, I think the telling will do you good. However, if you sense relational retreat after the telling, it will hurt very much. I suggest prayer and caution as well as courage."

Jill said, "Yeah, it's a huge risk. I've been thinking about it a lot. I don't know yet what I'll do. I don't want to lose his friendship, and yet I don't feel I've really got it unless he knows."

After Jill had nibbled to the core of her apple, she said, "Something else really great happened."

Nora's responsive "Let me in on it" was rewarded.

"There's a grad student who works in Holly's lab who told her about this apartment complex just on the edge of town, on Yosef Drive. They're mostly serious grad students living out there, and so it's not a rowdy party place. She and her roommates are moving out in late July, so their third story apartment will become available just when Holly, Megan and I would need a place. We went out and saw it last weekend. It is so great. It's three bedrooms and three bathrooms—How cool is that? It's not fancy or big, but it's in excellent condition and clean. It has a fully functional kitchen. There's a washer and dryer in the apartment. And best of all, the small living room has a big window with a terrific view. All the other places we could afford have been downright gloomy. And it is right next to an AppalCart stop. They said we can have it August 1, and our parents approve. I can't tell you how good it feels to know I'll have a clean and cheerful place to take care of my baby and study."

Nora commented, "God has certainly been in your details. The situation sounds perfect."

During their meeting they also discussed fetal development. Good news was confirmed that Robert Kelly's insurance would be covering Jill's maternity care. She had been a few times now to Watauga Obstetrics and Gynecology, which had been recommended by Mae at Promise.

Jill said, "I have a really nice midwife there; her name is Sanora. But I'll be having the baby with the Billinghams attending in Charlotte. Holly and my mom will coach me. I can't wait to revisit the birthing center there; I want so much to have the baby without any drugs. So far everything seems healthy and on schedule. I'm not due until two full weeks after my last final exam.

"I told Sanora that I don't want her to tell me the baby's sex after my ultrasound. I want to be surprised. When I go home at Christmas, I'm going to go to this huge thrift store for some baby things. The store supports Dr. Clery's school, and it always has tons of baby stuff really cheap. All the big, Catholic families around Charlotte trade their baby things around through it. I'll need a car seat, some diapers, and some clothes. I'm not big on pink, so even if she is a girl, I'd be going for the yellows and greens. If we keep on schedule, I'll earn a crib from Promise. Isn't that cool? I only have a twin bed in my room at home. So even though I like the idea of sleeping with the baby, we might be too crunched up. The thing I haven't figured out is how I'm going to pump my milk. I want to keep nursing after school starts, but Holly and Megan will need to bottle feed on Tuesdays and Thursdays."

Nora concluded that Jill's healthy nesting instincts were in operation. Realistic planning was an excellent sign.

Just before they left, Jill returned to the previous confusing subject. She thought aloud more than said, "Ted and my parents want to meet one another. Maybe I'll tell him about everything just before Thanksgiving break. If he doesn't pull back after I tell him, I'll introduce him to my parents when they come to pick me up for the holiday. If he does emotionally bail out, I could go home with God, my family, and Holly and Megan. I think I'd need my mom to deal with it."

"That might be a good idea," replied Nora.

Chapter 18

We have always developed both women and men as leaders. Our first president, Stacey Woods, set the tone: "His view of women in leadership was decades ahead of most other Christian leadership. Throughout the country, women staff workers were given the same assignments as men."

—Keith and Gladys Hunt, *For Christ and the University*

Shane Sayers, as an experienced director in InterVarsity, knew an important part of his calling was recognizing and discipling new church leadership. In Ted Mullins, Shane thought he saw a promising pastor and theologian. When Shane had been praying about how to help Ted develop his gifts, the thought of asking him to teach to the large-group had come quite clearly.

The older, but not that much older, man had read a few papers Ted had recently written. One had been on his interpretation of Genesis 2 and the foundation of gender equality. The other had been on the philosophical influence of Greek misogyny on the church fathers. It was hard to remember as he was reading them that they were written by a college freshman. The respect for scriptural authority and the unflinching intellectual integrity seemed to come from an elderly person of vast life experience. Ted was able to integrate historical evidence wisely and negotiate ideas insightfully to clearly explain the Scriptures. The papers exposed a gift for original organization and artful presentation necessary for excellent teaching. Ted's teaching was a flame Shane was determined to fan.

Shane also knew that he needed to do some teaching on women in the Pauline epistles. He now knew seven students, four women and three men, who were on the brink of accepting Christ, but for what they thought they saw as sexism in Paul's letters. He had been building relationships with them, answering questions, and teaching the gospel, but their misunderstanding, especially in a few of Paul's statements to Timothy and the church in Ephesus, created a stumbling block that prevented a final decision.

Just yesterday he had had coffee with Greg, a pre-law major. Greg told Shane that he knew he was a sinner, that the Bible just accounted for reality better than any other worldview he'd looked at, and that he desperately wanted his sins forgiven, but, he said, "If I really accept this, it looks like I'm supposed to treat and think about half the people in the world unjustly. If I go in for Christianity, I'll need to go in for the whole banana. If the Bible is true, it must all be true. Women aren't subhuman, so it doesn't look like the Bible is true."

Shane had countered with, "The Bible does not teach that women are subhuman."

Greg had then said, "Then you're going to need to tell me what the hell this passage does mean." He had then pointed out 1 Timothy 2:11–15.

Shane had first thought to give him Linda L. Belleville's "Teaching and Usurping Authority: 1 Timothy 2:11–15,"[1] but thought better of it. Greg was challenging him, and Shane was prompted to think he should take the challenge, even if Belleville was the better scholar. Shane decided he would teach on the passage first, and then give that article to Greg. Shane had simply said, "OK, before the end of the semester, I'll teach on that passage." Walking home from the coffeehouse to his apartment on Queen Street, Shane began to pray and think through how he might teach on 1 Timothy and give Ted Mullins an opportunity develop and recognize his gift. He felt the lessons were extremely important, for God may use them in saving students.

Shane thought about how arguments from nature were basic to hierarchical complementarity. To argue that view, he thought one must insist that patriarchy is normative. He remembered an example from Bruce Waltke's theology that he had photocopied. Was it in his backpack? No. But it did turn up in his jacket pocket. In his development of the order of creation Waltke had strongly supported the work of Steven Goldberg, and he had quoted Margaret Mead:

> The point that authority and leadership are, and always have been, associated with the male in every society, and I refer to this when I say that patriarchy is universal and that there has never been a matriarchy . . . Mead acknowledged that "It is true . . . that all the

---

1. In Pierce and Groothuis, *Discovering Biblical Equality*, 205–23.

Chapter 18

claims so glibly made about societies ruled by women are nonsense. We have no reason to believe that they ever existed."[2]

So the United Kingdom doesn't associate authority and leadership with Elizabeth I or Margaret Thatcher? India with Indira Gandhi and Patil? Are there no Condoleezza Rices, Sarah Palins, Hillary Clintons today? What about Kirchner, Sukhbaataryn Yanjmaa, Soong Ching-ling, de Peron, Bachelet, Tejada, Tizard, Sauve, Sirleaf, Bryce, Aquino, Rousseff, Bergmann-Pohl, Chamorro, Kinigi, Geun-hye, Kumaratunga, Serrano, McAleese, Arroyo? These are just some near the top of the list.

But even assuming it's a true generalization, Shane thought such a conclusion is what we should expect as a consequence of the curse in Genesis 3:16. In other words, no society has escaped the effects of the fall. Men will tend to domineer over women. If we generalize that men are often bigger and stronger than women, that women are usually the physically weaker vessel, that they are made especially vulnerable by the gestation and nursing of children, we see a source for the power of coercion. Shane thought such a state of affairs calls for redemptive action and continuing resistance to sin. Evidence of the curse deconstructs a justification for permanent gender-based hierarchy.

But this was not the biblical explanation being offered by Waltke. He gave a natural rationale in support of male leadership. His claim was that "nature tends to validate Scripture that men, not women, were created to lead."[3] But Shane thought, "Shouldn't we want our practice to be validated by Scripture? Perhaps we should say that it is natural in a fallen world? The essential question is, 'How does Scripture say we should relate to one another?'" Shane noticed that Waltke's interesting assertion came in the context of using a woman's authority (Mead's) to validate a man's authority (Goldberg's). Apparently women may be natural leaders in the field of anthropology. But of course Mead is a leader in the field not because she is a woman, but because she has remarkable gifts and talents in that area. So too in the church, women have parallel qualifications for leadership.

Shane thought that they must insist on the literal translation of 1 Timothy 3:11 which makes this perfectly clear. "Their wives" makes the character of the potential male deacons' wives a qualification for men serving the church. The preferable translation, "women" as in the NASB, shows that

---

2. Waltke, *Old Testament Theology*, 242, quoting Goldberg, *Why Men Rule: A Theory of Male Dominance* (Chicago: Open Court, 1993).

3. Waltke, *Old Testament Theology*, 242.

women's qualifications for leadership are almost identical to those of men. Giftedness and calling, not gender, are the qualifications for leadership.

Shane deemed Waltke's passionate rejection of the claim of matriarchal cultures in the quotation served to challenge the resurgence of goddess cults by contemporary secular feminists.[4] But as it stands, it leaves an oversimplified impression of ancient cultures. It ignores any relationship between the power of women in a culture and powerful female deities. Paganism imposes human characteristics, such as gender, upon its deities. And those who worship them become like them.

Shane thought about how women were seen as the source of life, and so, many ancient goddesses are the source of all creation. He felt Ted was up to the task of teaching about paganism on these points. Shane remembered that Tiamat's body was torn in two to become heaven and earth. While these goddesses may not have created a matriarchal culture by an anthropological definition, they did give women a certain power and respect, if not love. In ancient Sumer, for example, the female goddess Inanna was the most powerful deity of heaven and earth. The deity of the underworld was also female, Queen Ereshkigal. The merely human lover Dumuzi is practically voiceless in the myth and is banished by Inanna's decree to the underworld six months of the year to account for the seasons and the agricultural cycle.

We'll need to make the point that a key characteristic of paganism is gendered deities and that the postlapsarian battle of the sexes is reflected in the dysfunctional relationships among pagan gods. Pagan men and male deities tend to domineer through greater physical power, and women and female deities through their reproductive ability and sexual attraction. Our main point will be that when either sex domineers, discord results.

Shane appreciated how the true God of Scripture is unique at this point. This one true God is not made in the image of man (unlike the pagan deities and until the incarnation), but that man is made in the image of God. All humans are male or female, a limitation. Our God is infinite and beyond gender, but personal. Because humans cannot understand personality apart from gender, personal pronouns reflecting certain characteristics of our personal, infinite God are used in Scripture.

---

4. See works such as Carol P. Christ's *Rebirth of the Goddess: Finding Meaning in Feminist Spirituality* (Menlo Park: Addison-Wesley, 1997). Waltke is strongly supported in his claim about the nonexistence of matriarchal cultures by several recent works by Cynthia Eller. See, for example, *Gentlemen and Amazons: The Myth of Matriarchal Prehistory, 1861–1900* (Berkeley: University of California Press, 2011).

Chapter 18

We must not, therefore, think we may substitute one gendered pronoun or title for another. We ought not to say, "Our Mother who art in heaven," because it weakens our image of power and protection. But we must never minimize or ignore the ways in which our God is like a mother. We also need to know that our God is "as one whom his mother comforts."[5] Certainly male pronouns and images are more numerous, but the female ones are important and plentiful.

Moses appears to accept the paternal care of the Israelites; but it is one thing to lay down the law, and quite another to provide daily provision. For Moses, maternal care is utterly burdensome. Only God can give maternal care unaided. Moses' complaint implies that only God metaphorically conceives, begets, carries, and nurses the church.[6] God is the perfect father, but he is also the perfect mother. He has all the natural characteristics of both genders and, therefore, transcends gender.

> Can a woman forget her nursing child?
> And not have compassion on the son of her womb?
> Surely they may forget,
> Yet I will not forget you.[7]

Praise the Lord!

Much controversial ink has been spilt over the historical, gender climate and condition of New Testament Ephesus. Ted is up to teaching on that as well.

Perhaps I'll start with clear, uncontroversial passages that contradict Greg's interpretation, in other words start with what the passage cannot mean. Maybe we'll look at Deborah, Hulda, Anna, Priscilla, and Junia to show that women are praised elsewhere for teaching men. We'll also need to point out that verse 15 cannot mean that women are not "saved" in the sense of eternal salvation through childbirth, for the rest of the Scriptures are clear that women as well as men are "saved," in that sense, through the work of Christ.

The historical context leads quite logically into a discussion of genre and the one-sided nature of a letter. Historical context will provide several plausible problems that Paul may be speaking to Timothy about. Shane was

---

5. Isaiah 66:13.
6. Numbers 11:10–16.
7. Isaiah 49:15.

fully convinced that female dominance was that issue, but he did not want to be dogmatic about it. Ted could argue that point well.

The last angle he would address would be that of translation. Shane knew he would need to cover that himself, for Ted's Greek was only rudimentary. He would focus then on the "pejorative domineering over" of *authentein*. As he climbed his apartment steps, a flush of joy overwhelmed him. His Bible was indeed good news for women and men. The more he studied it, the more beautiful it became.

At IV large-group the next week, Jill heard Ted Mullins preach for the first time. The experience made her proud to be his friend. She knew he was helping others, because he was helping her. She desperately wanted to be accepted into her church and her future family for who she, as an individual, really was. She abhorred the idea of playing a role and longed to serve her Lord with all the gifts he had given her.

At IV Jill heard Ted say, "Most evangelical commentaries today do not even consider the influence of Artemis Ephesia on the young church in first-century Ephesus. That means they are not considering historical context. That goddess was the raison d'etre for that city for over seven thousand years. Until Christianity deconstructed her power, people flocked to worship her from all over the world. Her temple was the grandest building on earth, one of the great wonders of the ancient world, and the cause of Ephesian prominence and prosperity. The temple was marble with one hundred twenty-seven huge columns. It established the most secure bank in the world.

"Non-Christians trying to account for the rapid growth of Christianity in Ephesus point to the influence of Artemis. The Turkish archeologist and director of the Ephesus Museum, Selahattin Erdemgil, speaks the opinion of many scholars when he says that 'since the Virgin Mary possessed many of the virtues of Artemis, the most magnificent goddess, the new religion gained popularity in Ephesus and spread quickly.'[8]

"Now I think Christianity took root in Ephesus because it was true and because of the love in its community; but if I didn't, I would see these historians giving a very reasonable explanation.

"If I was a pregnant woman in a new house church and, according to my long-established culture, all I needed to do to ensure my safety and the safe delivery of my unborn child was to make a small offering to Artemis,

---

8. Erdemgil, *Ephesus*.

Chapter 18

I'd have been tempted. I hope I wouldn't have succumbed to idolatry, but I can't imagine Artemis wouldn't have tempted me.

"The superiority of female spirituality would also have been a temptation because my little church probably included not only the surrogate son John, but the Virgin Mary herself. The dominant cultural assumption of Ephesus was the superiority of female spirituality. Ephesus was the birthplace of Marian errors such as the immaculate conception of Mary in St. Anne, perpetual virginity, and the assumption of Mary. In Ephesus the third ecumenical council was called to counter Nestorius. In Ephesus "Theotokos" was first articulated. The first Christian church dedicated to the Virgin Mary was built at Ephesus. Female spiritual dominance must have been an influence upon the early church in Ephesus.

"When Domitian wanted to deify himself, he built his powerful statue in the shadow of the temple of Artemis. He needed to draw on her power, and he used that power to exile John. When Domitian was stabbed, it was to Ephesus that John returned to write his gospel. John is perhaps the apostle best suited to the gospel in Ephesus. He so strongly emphasizes his authoritative, eyewitness testimony, his theological metaphors, and his ideas about the love of God. Perhaps we should follow John's example in speaking to our own society that shares so many characteristics of pagan Ephesian culture."

Jill was convinced by his arguments. And she loved it when he said, "If I were a woman . . ." because he was assuming common human reactions. She also thought it pleasant that he was so handsome and had a sonorous voice.

After hearing Ted, Jill remembered her conviction that she was not gifted for public speaking. She knew she was good with ideas. She could think critically, and she was a devoted reader. She suspected God would use her voice in small intimate settings. But she would love to support his gifts for preaching, not because she was a woman and he was a man, but because she had her gifts and talents, and he had his. To be good at different things simply meant people needed each other. She determined to tell Ted why his sermon was so helpful to her and why she felt she saw a gift for preaching within him. She decided against telling him how handsome she thought he was or how she loved the mere sound of his voice.

Chapter 19

When a man gives his opinion, he's a man.
When a woman gives her opinion, she's a bitch.

—Bette Davis

November 12 at ten o'clock, Nora Shaw looked out at her world literature class and sighed. She had been handing back a take-home reading quiz on "Surat An-Nisa" of the *Qur'an*, and she had hoped to hand back Andrew Mitchell's paper to him before the official beginning of class. Disappointingly, he was late again. His quiz had been upsetting to her on two accounts.

First had been his attitude toward the subject. The surat dealt with Islamic teaching on women. And this reading assignment always brought forth a wide range of interpretation. Muslim students often wrote about how An-Nisa revealed a high view of women. Servat Kalpar's essay had been of this opinion. Many students could not bring themselves to say anything negative about another religion, and one read some interesting attempts to "explain away" passages such as 4:34. Jason Critcher had taken this route. Some students had a clear anti-Islamic bias, and did not give an honest reading. Matthew Okonkwo fell into this trap. One could clearly see his utter inability to any sort of objectivity. And Nora knew why; three of his cousins had been murdered by Boko Haram only last year. Some students did very careful readings and concluded the text was sexist. Both Ted Mullins and Dana Blevin arrived at this conclusion through good scholarship.

But Drew's paper had been the worst of all worlds. His essay implied he had not read the assignment, had assumed it was sexist, and had sympathized with violence against women. At several points in his essay, the writing style had suddenly changed as did the font from cut-and-paste moves. When the professor had googled the borrowed, uncited language, she was taken to a disgusting, misogynous website. The title of the site was

Chapter 19

"Frats in the Bro Code," and it was an obvious supporter of rape culture and male dominance of all sorts. Dr. Shaw had filled out the obligatory Student Misconduct Report, and given him an F on the assignment for his plagiarism. The Office of Student Conduct required the student to sign the report, which Dr. Shaw had stapled to Drew's quiz. She was not sure how he would respond, so she decided to hand the rest of the papers back at the end of class. For some reason she could not rule out Drew causing a scene over this.

Dr. Shaw received few plagiarized papers, and when she did she was always disappointed. It was a breach of academic integrity, and she always challenged the student. Almost always the student had been under serious, if not impossible, time pressure and had, under this stress, made an unethical decision. When confronted, they were generally embarrassed, humbled, and apologetic. In spite of the F she always gave on the assignment, these students were usually eager to win back her respect and would work very hard the rest of the semester. Because of the professor's firm but gentle and forgiving treatment of the problem, she sometimes became a favorite of these offenders for this very reason. She had no problem continuing to like them.

She wasn't expecting that usual response from Drew. She was uncomfortable with anticipating "the worst." No matter how Drew took the bad news, she decided to run her feelings past Eric, her department head.

After class, she asked Drew to stay a moment. He came up and waited impatiently at her podium while she gave the other latecomer his quiz. When she handed the paper to Drew, he glanced over it just long enough to realize what it was and then crumpled it up in his angry fist and said, "This is bullshit!" He stormed out of the room without another word. She thought, "Yep, definitely time to run this student past Eric."

That afternoon nobody was in her office at the close of office hours. Nora headed for Eric's office. From the hall she could see him in his large inner office, but she stopped at Tim's desk in the outer office and asked, "Is Eric frantically busy?"

Tim said, "He's heading out to a meeting in about ten minutes—If it's quick?"

Nora replied, "I only need a couple minutes. Thanks." She stuck her head in the big office and asked, "Eric, sorry to interrupt. Do you have a second?"

This was the first time Nora had had a serious problem with a student at Blue Ridge, and she wondered how her new department head would react to her situation. She had a student at Cal Poly with anger management issues, and her head there had been very glad for what he had called a "heads up." That department head had given her the support she had hoped for.

Although his back was turned, and he was reading the agenda for the coming meeting, he answered, "Come on in, Nora. What's up?" And by that time, he had turned toward her, sat down, and motioned for her to do the same.

"I just wanted you to know that I'm not getting along very well with one of my 2030 students." She briefly explained Drew's quiz, her actions, and his response. She ended with, "I just don't have a good feeling here."

Eric said, "I know that you are new here, but you have followed our procedures exactly. You have, moreover, acted wisely. I imagine I would feel just as you do about this student if I were in your shoes... At present I suspect that he may be the sort of character who would calm down better by a word from the 'Boss Man.' Emphasis is on the word 'man,' but this is entirely up to you. If you want to negotiate this by yourself, you have my support and permission. I only suggest that we may avoid unpleasantness in your classroom if I talk to this particular brand of disrespect myself. Male power is sometimes stifled by male power where it is enflamed by female power. I am not pulling rank over you, but offering to pull it over your student in support of you. It is your call. As you know, Nora, I'm a Hemmingway scholar. I, therefore, have some understanding of a masculine ego."

"Thanks Eric, I'd appreciate you having a 'man-to-man' with Drew Mitchell. Normally, I would want to work into the relationship myself, but I don't think we have enough of a foundation to work from. I just want you to know that I will keep very accurate grades on him, and be absolutely fair about what he earns."

"I expect that you will. You always have since you've been here. I've got to go, but please keep me in the loop on Mr. Mitchell. I'll email you after we have our chat."

"Thanks so much, Eric, I feel I'm part of a team for the real benefit of all these 'characters.'"

"And the team is very glad to have you as a player. I consider this conversation as evidence of mutual trust, and that is the basis upon which I desire to administer this department. My line of communication is open. Thank you, Nora."

"Thank you, Eric."

Chapter 19

As she exited the huge, double glass doors, with a feeling of relief, she thought about Avery Hall as a thriving subculture. It was a community focused on texts and talking about them. It nourished young minds in the fertile soil of ideas. Twenty yards from the building she stopped and turned round to look at it. "Nothing to get architecturally excited about, nothing but an old brick building"—And yet, she thought, "It has enough glass." From her third floor office, she looked down on Avery Mall at the heart of the university, a hub of student life. The glass doors were important. The subculture of texts provided a vision of the wider culture. The bricks provided the necessary protection, and the glass the connection to life in a culture with little interest in old texts. To exit the glass doors of Avery was to take the ideas in texts into all of life. It was not an ivory tower to Nora, but a necessary vision of reality. Drew's plagiarism and disrespect violated that subculture and reminded Nora that the world was indeed sadly fallen—No news, but always disappointing. Today she did not want to carry the ideas out of Avery. In spite of her deep humility toward the text, and her ignorance of Arabic, she did not like "An-Nisa," in spite of the greatness of its poetry. It was an incredibly influential text, and that was why she included it on her syllabus. The text accurately reflected an aspect of gender relationships needing discussion. But Drew liked "An-Nisa" probably without even reading it, and that was what troubled her most.

Nora headed toward Expresso Yosef for a meeting with Jill. She lacked her usual enthusiasm for the meeting. She felt tired and dispirited, despite Eric's sound support. The gloomy, grey day was melting isolated and muddy patches of snow. She was seeing Jill in sad consequence of violent male dominance, and she did not feel like facing it again. But Nora had committed to the appointment, so she sincerely, if lethargically, prayed, "Oh, God—Your strength in my weakness," and trudged doggedly on. Today Nora wished she were heading for a big, relaxing glass of old vine Zinfandel from the Central Coast rather than a proverbial cup of joe.

Pushing the funky door of the coffeehouse open, her senses were welcomed by an indistinct buzz of a dozen conversations merging with the knocking of damp espresso grounds out of filters. An aroma of baking scones and a Kenyan medium roast mixed and filled the air. Because she remembered to say "for here" rather than "to go," she felt in her hands a warm, grainy, hand-thrown, glazed mug instead of a paper cup. The mild state of dilapidation relaxed her almost as much as the zin would have. At the top of the stairs, in their corner, waited Jill.

Nora greeted her warmly, and Jill, taking a sip of her smoothie, didn't seem to notice the taint of emotional exhaustion in her smile. Jill offered her the armchair, and Nora collapsed into it. "I can care and listen," thought Nora, "and that is all I have to offer today." But apparently that was all that Jill needed from her. For almost an hour, Nora uttered not a word. Her body language was in working order, and she could sympathetically grunt or sigh. Such were adequate pieces of evidence to Jill that Nora cared and was listening.

"Guess what?" demanded Jill.

(Questioning grunt)

"Last Friday Ted and I had lunch together in the Profile Trail Lounge in the PSU. We were just sitting there after we finished eating. And he asked me as softly as velvet, 'Jill, are you pregnant?' I knew it wasn't really a question. He knew, and had known, that I was. He already knew and had still befriended me. He wanted me to tell him about how."

(Sympathetic sigh)

"I told Ted everything. I told him about Holly meeting Kevin Parsons. I told him every detail I remember of the frat party. I told him about the morning at the hospital. I told him about all that the detective found out and all the upsetting questions he asked. I told him about running too much. I even told him that he was the only guy I talked to in weeks. I told him about having a mentor at Promise. Best of all I thanked him for reaching out to me, knowing as he did from the beginning."

(Ahhhh)

"I felt it impossible to hold anything back from him. And so I told him I had wanted to tell him everything for a long time, but that I was afraid he would withdraw from our friendship. Do you know what he said?"

(Wide-eyed shake of the head)

"Nothing, he said nothing. He just very gently but firmly picked up my hand and kissed it. When he did that, tears just started pouring out of my eyes. My tears didn't make him a bit uncomfortable; he was grieving for me . . . and for Holly and for Megan. He just sat there saying nothing and holding my hand like he wouldn't mind holding it forever."

(Mmmm, with tears)

"He and Holly and Megan are such amazing friends. God is so good to me. And here you are caring and listening. I want sooo much to go to church and worship Him, but I do not want to buy into one ounce of male dominance. I need to be pure from that; I've had enough of it.

Chapter 19

"I really do not think I bore any guilt for the rape. But I was totally responsible for the shame. God forgave and accepted me. He approved of me, but somehow that wasn't good enough for me. I've been holding on to the shame."

(Deep, smooth guttural)

"Ted keeps telling me in many ways that Jesus died for my guilt and my shame. Not too long after the frat party, I felt free of guilt. But that heavy, heavy shame has been weighing me down. I'm committed now, with God's help, to off-loading it. This week we told each other we'd memorize Hebrews 12:1–2. I'm going to become a champion 'shame-despiser' as I already have been a runner.

> Wherefore seeing we also are compassed about with so great a cloud of witnesses, let us lay aside every weight, and the sin which doth so easily beset us, and let us run with patience the race that is set before us, looking unto Jesus the author and finisher of our faith; who for the joy that was set before him endured the cross, despising the shame, and is set down at the right hand of the throne of God.

"You know what?"

(Another wide-eyed shake of the head)

"Ted said he knew I was pregnant the first night we talked at IV. He even told his mom. They all accepted me anyway, and it's not because they don't care about sexual purity. He and his family are just plain loving."

(A nod of agreement)

"I was so gutsy. I told him that I was constantly bothered by the idea that if I ever got married, my husband wouldn't be my first sexual partner. I wanted to be a virgin on my wedding night. You know what he said?"

(Return to the wide-eyed shake of the head)

"He said he thought a partnership involves mutual consent. Since I did not give consent, I have never had a sexual partner. He told me that I talked like I am somehow damaged goods. Any man who loves me will see that my suffering has matured my character and my relationship with God, and will appreciate those things more than untouched skin. Don't you think Ted is amazing?"

(A smiling nod)

"Nora, this dumping shame may be a pretty long and difficult process. It's really hard and scary. But I feel comfortable trusting Ted. He has taken away my fear of exposure. He's a guy about the same age as 'whoever it was.'

He was a stranger, just as 'whoever it was' was a stranger. And Ted is kind and trustworthy. Can you imagine how wonderful that is?"

(A soft, bilabial sigh)

"Even if Ted disappeared tomorrow, and I sure hope he doesn't; I would know that a guy like him exists. When you look at a television, listen to the radio, see a magazine, or experience our culture in a million other ways; you are told that men think of women as objects for their sexual pleasure—full stop. A group rape conclusively proves it is often true. Ted proves that it can be a lie. If a Ted exists, it's easy for me to believe there are others out there like him. Isn't it great how one person's goodness can change the world for others? Don't you think Ted would be an excellent pastor? He's smart, and he would do his sermon homework. But he can use his Bible to show people why they should hope. He can bring God's love to bear on how they feel. He makes trusting God the only sensible approach. He can show people something of how God loves them."

Finally Nora was empowered to speak. "Is all that because Ted is such an extraordinary person?"

Jill slowed down . . . She thought, "How could anyone question whether Ted was an extraordinary person?" But after thinking the question over, she said, "He's filled with God's love; all his goodness comes from God. But God has sure made him lovable."

Chapter 20

...He was even calling God his own Father, making himself equal with God.
—John 5:18

Have this mind among yourselves, which is yours in Christ Jesus, who... did not count equality with God a thing to be grasped, but emptied himself, by taking the form of a servant...
—Philippians 2:6

Nora was again wearing her Sorels to work. Yesterday four inches of snow had fallen, and the world was white. Descending through the forest behind the football stadium, she prayed, "Purifying Lord, please make my heart as clean as this, not mixed with mud on the edge of the road, but stacked high on the branches of evergreens, clinging to your life."

Today would be her last day for a week. Tomorrow she would take a flight from Charlotte to Birmingham then catch a train to Shrewsbury to spend the night. Day after tomorrow she would arrive at Gregynog to attend an academic conference with her "Herbert friends." She would be speaking on the superiority of oral metaphors for the Trinity in seventeenth-century devotional poetry.

To her the subject seemed super relevant, but nobody except other scholars in her field seemed to care. To her the relationship of persons in the Trinity provided a perfect model for human relationships. After the Enlightenment one came across so many tiresome visual metaphors for the Trinity which destroyed the interpenetration of relationship. Visual metaphors seemed to produce an image in which the Trinity was separated according to different functions. When Nora looked carefully for this idea in her Bible, she just could not find it. It was easier for her to imagine the Trinity as three personal voices in perfect harmony. They shared functions such as creation and comfort. They resonated with one another. They were multiple persons whose wills were merged into a common single will. When she and Luke deeply agreed and acted with a single purpose, weren't they like God in some small way? The thought brought to her mind Herbert's "Easter."

> Rise heart; thy Lord is risen. Sing his praise
>   Without delayes,
> Who takes thee by the hand, that thou likewise
>   With him mayst rise:
> That, as his death calcined thee to dust,
> His life may make thee gold, and much more, just.
>
> Awake, my lute, and struggle for thy part
>   With all thy art.
> The crosse taught all wood to resound his name,
>   Who bore the same.
> His stretched sinews taught all strings, what key
> Is best to celebrate this most high day.
>
> Consort both heart and lute, and twist a song
>   Pleasant and long:
> Or, since all musick is but three parts vied
>   And multiplied;
> O let thy blessed Spirit bear a part,
> And make up our defects with his sweet art.[1]

    Nora's conference attendance would necessitate cancelling three meetings of her Monday, Wednesday, Friday classes. Conferences were the only reason she had ever cancelled classes. Blessed with excellent health, she had not ever needed to cancel because of illness. But she felt an occasional conference an important element to maintaining quality teaching. It inspired her own writing and research, and it was the only opportunity outside the classroom for her work to be a social experience. She loved hearing about what other Herbert scholars were thinking and doing. At Blue Ridge she could talk about pedagogy with her colleagues, but none of them were particularly interested in early seventeenth-century devotional poetry.

    She thought about what assignments she had planned for her ten o'clock 2030 class. Wednesday, November 13, she would have them write a take-home quiz on Augustine's *Confessions*. November 15, Friday, they

---

    1. Herbert, *English Poems*, 139–40.

Chapter 20

would meet in groups to peer edit their medieval essays. Monday, November 18, they would write a one-page essay on the Christianization of the Pagan in *Beowulf*. She was satisfied that even in her absence, her students would have a productive week. For Friday's peer editing, she had, for the first time, assigned the peer editing groups. Students choose the text they would write on, and she had put students together who were writing on the same text. The students would certainly not complain about not having to attend class for a week.

At ten o'clock on Friday, November 15, while Nora Shaw was giving a paper in Wales on metaphors for the Trinity, conversations on various medieval texts were occurring all over Poplar, North Carolina. Rachel and Crystal were giggling over *The Second Shepherds' Play* by the Wakefield Master at the Local Lobo coffeehouse. Servat Kalpar and Matthew Okonkwo were discussing Du Fu's *To My Retired Friend Wei* on the third floor of the Belk Library. Jason Critcher and Travis Williams were arguing over the symbolism in *Sir Gawain and the Green Knight* in the second floor common room of the Eggers residence hall. Andrew Mitchell and Ted Mullins sat at the dining table in Drew's fraternity house on Orchard Street debating the character of Chaucer's Wife of Bath.

Andrew said, "She proves every feminine trait in the book. She henpecks all her husbands, marries for money, has a voracious sexual appetite, is preoccupied with how she looks, and just uses men. If we didn't need sex and kids, we could do without them."

Ted on the other hand, rather adored her. He saw in her a fun and sympathetic character, whose negative attributes had been developed by the men in her life. He said, "Her dad had her marry an old man when she was but a teenager—for his money. And it worked. It's no wonder she's willing to marry for money. I can certainly imagine her getting sick and tired of hearing Jankyn read his nasty book. She seems quite willing to serve her husbands when they quit struggling for power over her. I think both her prologue and her tale show us that as soon a husband willingly gives up sovereignty, maybe his wife will give it up too."

Drew quietly disrespected Ted for his rejection of what Drew thought of as the "Bro Code." He and his frat brothers enjoyed a camaraderie that he could never share with this wimp. Tonight was Friday night, and they'd rock.

Ted wasn't noticing the coldness of Drew's silence and body language. Something was unusual about a bottle of nasal spray on the kitchen counter sitting next to a punchbowl. He was preoccupied by a vehicle he had just seen park across Orchard Street from the *Beta Alpha Delta* house. It was a black 2013 GMC panel van, and the custom license plate said MAL DOM.

Ted did not have his cell phone, but when he returned to Mullins Mountain about thirty minutes later, he called Detective Steve Konnenburg at the Poplar Police Department and told him everything that he had seen.

Chapter 21

Does a rake deserve to possess anything of worth, since he chases everything in skirts and then imagines he can successfully hide his shame by slandering [women in general]?

—Christine de Pizan, *The Letter of the God of Love*

At nine o'clock Thursday morning, November 21, Nora's return flight from Birmingham touched down at Charlotte/Douglass International Airport. An intercom announcement preparing the passengers for landing had awakened her from a deep sleep. She usually could not sleep during flights, but she must have dozed off soon after take-off. The transatlantic flight seemed to have taken just a few minutes. "Now this is the way to travel," she congratulated herself. By nine-thirty she had found her Subaru in the long-term lot and was heading north on the Billy Graham Parkway. She had not taken a cell phone with her to the UK, but Luke always wanted her to have one in the car whenever she was driving out of Poplar by herself. She blue-toothed Luke. When he picked up, she said, "Hey Hon, I'm safely back on American soil. I slept almost all the way home. This direct flight from Birmingham to Charlotte makes Mid Wales a breeze. How are you?"

"Better now that you're back. You should be in Poplar by eleven-thirty this morning, but I can't possibly get there until about five o'clock. How 'bout I take you out to Tamarind to celebrate your return? Don't bother to cook dinner. I'll pick you up at the house about five. How does that sound?"

"Have you ever known me to turn down Indian food? I can't wait to see you again. I wish you could have come with me; It was a great conference."

"I bet your paper went over well."

"I did get some good feedback and an offer for a chapter contribution."

"I'm not a bit surprised."

"Anything unusual happen at SR while I was gone?"

"Not really, Dave and Mason are the only ones deployed. They're at a flood in Cleveland. William and I are next out, but no disasters are brewing that we know of."

"Great, we should have the whole weekend together," she said cheerfully.

He said, "Too bad we've both got to work tomorrow. I feel like an early start on this weekend."

"We've got tonight and the weekend—Things could be worse."

"I'm so glad you're home. Things get dull quickly when you aren't around . . . I've got a meeting in two minutes."

"I should give my attention to traffic ahead. See ya soon."

"Thanks for calling right away; I was gearing up to worry. Bye."

On the other side of a traffic jam on the 85, Nora pressed her audio button. She forgot what she had left in the machine. She heard, "Recorded Books presents *Cry, the Beloved Country* by Alan Paton, copyright 1948 by Alan Paton. This recording is copyright 1992 by Recorded Books, Incorporated, and is narrated by Maggie Soboil." By the time Stephen Kumalo met his son's pregnant girlfriend, Nora was in Poplar.

It was then Nora noticed how hungry she was. She swung into the Baguette Boy parking lot, went in and purchased a peanut butter and banana smoothie and a brioche roll. Exiting the bakery, see looked across the highway and saw Avery Hall beckoning. She knew she had left everything in order for tomorrow morning, but she couldn't even remember what the reading assignments were. "Maybe I should stop by the office for a few minutes, refresh myself on tomorrow's lesson plans and get a head start on the inevitable email backlog. I'll still have plenty of time to unpack and take a nice long bath before Luke gets home," she thought. She could even see an empty parking space, a positive omen.

She drove across the street and parked in the Locust lot. First thing inside her office, she pushed the button on her computer. While it was booting up, she peeked in her 2030 portfolio. She thought, "Oh now I remember, the first day on *Journey to the West* by Wu Cheng'en." Students always loved the Buddhist epic novel. In the 2050 portfolio she saw her introductory material for Kipling's *Kim*. She would hate to separate from Luke for the day after being gone for a week, but tomorrow would still be a fun day.

She clicked on Microsoft Outlook and up came her inbox. She clicked on an email from Eric dated the day she left.

Chapter 21

Dear Nora,

I'm sorry to say my little chat with Mr. Andrew Mitchell did not go well this morning. For example, when I mentioned that plagiarism was a serious offense, He said (and I quote), "It's no big deal. The woman is just on a power trip." Mr. Mitchell was actually surprised that I did not share his attitude. I intend to do some research into this matter. I would prefer that you not return to your ten o'clock English 2030 class before we talk again.

Sincerely,

Eric

Scrolling up, she came across another email from Eric, this one dated Friday, November 15. The time was two o'clock p.m.

Dear Nora,

My opinion of Mr. Mitchell continues to deteriorate. It seems he lied about prior criminal activity on his admissions application. Although your student's SAT scores are sky high and his father gives stacks of money to the Mountaineer Football program, he looks like a very dangerous character to me. I had told you decisions about him would be your own. But, after consulting with both the Dean of Students and the Associate Vice Chancellor for Equity, I'm taking the matter out of your hands. Please do not talk about this with anybody yet, but I will be administratively removing Mr. Mitchell from your class. Indeed, I don't want him setting foot in Avery Hall ever again. I'll keep you posted.

Sincerely,

Eric

Nora scrolled up only a few inches before seeing another email from Eric. It was from Saturday, November 16.

Dear Nora,

My dealings with Mr. Mitchell the past two days have involved the Poplar Police, and he is presently incarcerated in the Watauga County Jail. He will be staying in those lodgings until the police get some results from a forensic lab. Also in jail is Andrew's older brother, John Mitchell. And connections to your ten o'clock 2030 continue. Your student Mr. Theodore Mullins has been very useful to the police in this matter. He seems to have very observantly identified an important vehicle in the case, and had previous knowledge of key details of the crime which he put to intelligent use. A drug rape victim in Cone Hall identified John Mitchel by his alias Stephen Carrigan. A drug rape victim in Summit Hall identified John Mitchell by his alias Wayne Branton. Two women residing in Gorman Hall have positively identified John Mitchell by his alias Kevin Parsons. Police are reluctant to let the accused see a third victim in that crime. I am not sure why. Your bringing Mr. Andrew Mitchell to my attention, my little research and consultation with two administrators, and especially your clever student Mr. Mullins, have been very helpful to the police and have most likely made BRSU a significantly safer place for our female students.

Sincerely,

Eric

Monday, November 18, Eric posted another email.

Dear Nora,

Results from the forensic lab have not only confirmed the guilt of Andrew and John Mitchell, but have sent the entire Beta Alpha Delta fraternity to jail along with them. The police are also thrilled to have arrested a certain devilishly brilliant assistant in the chemistry lab, who has been creating high-quality rape drugs. We are so glad to have ended his thriving business. It seems the plethora of forensic evidence will, most likely, along with the criminals' own statements, free many girls from needing to testify in painful trails. Today, if not every day, justice has been served. Thank you most heartily for bringing my attention to your student's "character."

Sincerely,

Eric

That evening at Tamarind over samosas, tandoori shrimp, chicken tikka masala, biryani rice, garlic nan, and kheer for dessert, Luke and Nora had plenty to eat and plenty to talk about.

Chapter 22

Grant that the bonds of our common humanity, by which all your children are united one to another, and the living to the dead, may be so transformed by your grace, that your Will may be done on earth as it is in heaven; where, O Father, with your Son, and the Holy Spirit, you live and reign in perfect unity, now and forever. *Amen.*

—BOOK OF COMMON PRAYER[1]

CORMAC BRUCE'S BUSINESS CARD had, not many Sundays after its offering, led Nora and Luke to visit King of Kings Anglican Church. They had immediately connected with the community. Although it was small and depended for its organization on a somewhat disorganized Pastor Bruce, it was alive with faith, full of people who really trusted and loved their Redeemer. Cormac, while not an administrator, was more importantly a genuine shepherd and scholarly teacher. The church did not have enough musicians for accompaniment every week, and the hotel conference room didn't provide quite the right ambiance for the Eucharist. It was, nevertheless, an excellent spiritual home. Luke and Nora integrated quickly into the life of the small congregation. Kyle's family had come to spend the Easter vacation with his parents, and they had liked King of Kings also. Blythe's family had visited for a week in July and agreed that Mom and Dad had found a healthy church.

Two couples had become particular favorites of the Shaws. And Nora had been delighted to discover that both were related to Ted from her ten o'clock world lit class. She and Luke found themselves close friends with the very Uncle Hank, professor of computer science, with whom Ted rode in to school, and his wife, Aunt Kathy. Hank and Kathy Mullins shared a sea of interests with Nora and Luke Shaw. The old grandmother, now Nora's

---

1. All liturgical language in this chapter is based upon the *Book of Common Prayer*, 1662, by the Church of England.

friend Hannah, and the old grandfather of the clan, Tom Mullins, were founding members of King of Kings. Hannah was particularly well-read and very eager about discussing literature with Nora. When Nora had suspected their connection to her student, she had said nothing to them. She always maintained strict confidentiality with her students. If Ted wanted his family to know about his relationship with his professor, he would need to tell them.

But the next Sunday after she had suspected they were Ted's extended family, right after the service, Hannah approached Nora and said, "This week my grandson, Ted, and I put two and two together and concluded that you are the professor of the literature class that he's been raving about. You have wholly succeeded in sending him down some new intellectual trails, and his head is now quite full of Oxford. Tom and I have almost decided to help his folks foot the bill if he is admitted. Indeed, we're all rather excited about it. He tells me you're writing him an excellent recommendation."

"I am. And none of it is beyond his desert. He's a top student, and you have sufficient cause to be very proud of him."

"Thanks for saying so. We have tried to look after his education. But you know it's his faith and character which particularly please us. Of course, he's a sinner like the rest of us, but unlike so many—he knows it. He also knows that Jesus took care of his problem. He seems to know these things more deeply than many nineteen-year-olds. Our good God has been at work."

That conversation occurred many weeks ago, but Nora remembered it well as she and Luke walked across the icy hotel parking lot in early January. As usual they were some of the first King of Kingers to arrive. Most Sundays, including today, they went to an eight-fifteen service at the large Poplar Bible Fellowship before driving directly over to the hotel. At PBF they worshipped with an excellent praise band and heard good preaching. They usually arrived about 9:50 for the ten o'clock service at King of Kings, but it never seemed to actually start at ten.

Through the double doors they entered the warm lobby. At the far end of that high-ceilinged room they turned left at the breakfast room to the smell of waffles baking and warm maple syrup. When they came to the door to the indoor pool, they turned right and entered the conference room. Beatrice Edgars and her father, Jerry, today's musicians, were warming up, she on the keyboard and he on the guitar. Luke retrieved a beautiful banner from the corner and hung it on the wall behind the "altar," which

Chapter 22

was foldup banquet table draped with a plain linen cloth. Nora took their usual chairs near the front and gestured to Luke to help him get the banner level. Next Darcy and Dick arrived, and she artistically arranged a simple wooden cross, candlesticks, and the communion service on the altar. She also put a little offering basket, which was never passed round, in the far corner. At 10:02 Carolyn Claymore arrived with a gorgeous arrangement of dahlias, and the altar was now ready. Nora wondered how Carolyn could possibly come up with such a wonder in January. By 10:03 several families with young children were seated and fidgeting already in the back. King of Kings had no nursery or Sunday School, so members of the congregation who could be counted on to sit still sat toward the front. At 10:04 Pastor Bruce arrived with three of his five children. His wife, Nora assumed, must be home with their infant twins. His son, Joshua, quickly walked through the rows of stackable chairs laying a prayer book bulletin on every second chair. At 10:07 Luke and Nora connected to the church universal and entered the liturgy with Pastor Bruce and their friends.

First Beatrice and Jerry led them in singing, and by the sound Nora knew the conference room was very full. The church may not be punctual, but neither was it very late.

> The church's one foundation
> is Jesus Christ her Lord;
> she is his new creation
> by water and the Word.
> From heaven he came and sought her
> to be his holy bride;
> with his own blood he bought her,
> and for her life he died.
>
> Elect from every nation,
> yet one o'er all the earth;
> her charter of salvation,
> one Lord, one faith, one birth;
> one holy name she blesses,
> partakes one holy food,
> and to one hope she presses,
> with every grace endued.
>
> Though with a scornful wonder
> we see her sore oppressed,
> by schisms rent asunder,

by heresies distressed,
yet saints their watch are keeping;
their cry goes up, "How long?"
And soon the night of weeping
shall be the morn of song.

Mid toil and tribulation,
and tumult of her war,
she waits the consummation
of peace forevermore;
till, with the vision glorious,
her longing eyes are blest,
and the great church victorious
shall be the church at rest.

Yet she on earth hath union
with God the Three in One,
and mystic sweet communion
with those whose rest is won.
O happy ones and holy!
Lord, give us grace that we
like them, the meek and lowly,
on high may dwell with thee.[2]

Next they read Psalm 127 antiphonally. Nora remembered how this psalm had worked a revolution in Jill's attitude toward God's purpose in her pregnancy, toward her unborn child, and on her decision to parent her baby. Nora prayed that it might work upon herself now.

Unless the Lord builds the house,
They labor in vain who build it;
Unless the Lord guards the city,
The watchman keeps awake in vain.
It is vain for you to rise up early,
To retire late,
To eat the bread of painful labors;
For He gives to His beloved even in his sleep.

Behold, children are a gift of the Lord,
The fruit of the womb is a reward.
Like arrows in the hand of a warrior,
So are the children of one's youth.

---

2. Samuel Wesley, 1864, and Samuel J. Stone, 1868.

Chapter 22

> How blessed is the man whose quiver is full of them;
> They will not be ashamed
> When they speak with their enemies in the gate.

Then all the people stood and Cormac said, "Blessed be God: Father, Son, and Holy Spirit. And blessed be his kingdom, now and forever. Amen."

This congregation loved both the meaning and beauty of the dear old words, and most people had them long since memorized. New people followed the prayer book bulletins. Familiarity with the prayer had not desensitized this congregation to their sins. Together they prayed:

"Most merciful God, we confess that we have sinned against you in thought, word, and deed, by what we have done, and by what we have left undone. We have not loved you with our whole heart; we have not loved our neighbor as ourselves. We are truly sorry and we humbly repent. For the sake of your Son, Jesus Christ, have mercy on us and forgive us; that we may delight in your will, and walk in your ways, to the glory of your Name. Amen."

The pastor sat down, and gave his congregation some time to offer their individual confessions; then he said, "Hear what our Lord Jesus Christ saith: Thou shalt love the Lord thy God with all thy heart, and with all thy soul, and with all thy mind. This is the first and great commandment. And the second is like unto it: Thou shalt love thy neighbor as thyself. On these two commandments hang all the Law and the Prophets.

"Almighty God, our heavenly Father, who of His great mercy has promised forgiveness of sins to all who with hearty repentance and true faith turn to him, have mercy upon you, pardon and deliver you from all your sins, confirm and strengthen you in all goodness, and bring you to everlasting life; through Jesus Christ our Lord. Amen"

Beatrice and Jerry immediately began and all joined in singing.

> Holy God,
> Holy and Mighty,
> Holy Immortal One,
> Have mercy upon us.

Then Cormac prayed, "O God the Father of our Lord Jesus Christ, our only Savior, the Prince of Peace: Give us grace seriously to lay to heart the great dangers we are in by our unhappy divisions; take away all hatred and prejudice, and whatever else may hinder us from godly union and concord; that, as there is but one Body and one Spirit, one hope of our calling, one

Lord, one Faith, one Baptism, one God and Father of us all, so we may be all of one heart and of one soul, united in one holy bond of truth and peace, of faith and charity, and may with one mind and one mouth glorify you; through Jesus Christ our Lord. Amen."

Cormac said, "The Lord be with you."

The people responded with, "And with thy spirit." Then the people sat down, and Luke went forward to read. His clear, sensitive lector-voice began. "The Old Testament lesson is from the second chapter of Genesis, verses eighteen through twenty-five."

Startled, Nora looked at Luke. She wasn't sure whether this was the first or second Sunday after the Epiphany, but she thought, "Shouldn't Luke be reading from Isaiah?"

> And the Lord God said, "It is not good that man should be alone; I will make him a helper comparable to him." Out of the ground the Lord God formed every beast of the field and every bird of the air, and brought them to Adam to see what he would call them. And whatever Adam called each living creature, that was its name. So Adam gave names to all cattle, to the birds of the air, and to every beast of the field. But for Adam there was not found a helper comparable to him.
>
> And the Lord God caused a deep sleep to fall on Adam, and he slept; and He took one of his ribs, and closed up the flesh in its place. Then the rib which the Lord God had taken from man He made into a woman, and He brought her to the man. And Adam said:
>
>> "This is now bone of my bones
>> And flesh of my flesh;
>> She shall be called Woman,
>> Because she was taken out of Man."
>
> Therefore a man shall leave his father and mother and be joined to his wife, and they shall become one flesh. And they were both naked, the man and his wife, and were not ashamed . . .

"The Epistle is from the sixteenth chapter of Romans, verses one through twenty."

Again Nora questioned Luke's accuracy. She thought, "Romans doesn't come up till Lent." It wasn't that she was disappointed; she adored Romans sixteen and especially when it was just read through. Sure it was encouraging that Priscilla was Apollos' teacher. And pastors who tried to

Chapter 22

explain away Junia as an apostle were always entertaining, but it was the overall tone that made her so deeply happy. To Nora it wasn't just a boring list of odd-sounding names, but the generous inclusion of women, without any explanation or justification whatsoever. Paul so obviously and naturally included women in ministry. Nora's favorite phrases were "fellow worker in Christ," "laborer in the Lord," "servant of the church" and such like, depending on the translation. Paul did not send the ladies off to the women's Bible study to play church. Not he, he worked shoulder to shoulder with them and included them just like other people, presupposing they actually belonged in a diverse list of commendable saints.

> I commend to you our sister Phoebe, who is a servant of the church which is at Cenchrea; that you receive her in the Lord in a manner worthy of the saints, and that you help her in whatever matter she may have need of you; for she herself has also been a helper of many, and of myself as well.
>
> Greet Prisca and Aquila, my fellow workers in Christ Jesus, who for my life risked their own necks, to whom not only do I give thanks, but also all the churches of the Gentiles; also greet the church that is in their house. Greet Epaenetus, my beloved, who is the first convert to Christ from Asia. Greet Mary, who has worked hard for you. Greet Andronicus and Junias, my kinsmen and my fellow prisoners, who are outstanding among the apostles, who also were in Christ before me. Greet Ampliatus, my beloved in the Lord. Greet Urbanus, our fellow worker in Christ, and Stachys my beloved. Greet Apelles, the approved in Christ. Greet those who are of the household of Aristobulus. Greet Herodion, my kinsman. Greet those of the household of Narcissus, who are in the Lord. Greet Tryphaena and Tryphosa, workers in the Lord. Greet Persis the beloved, who has worked hard in the Lord. Greet Rufus, a choice man in the Lord, also his mother and mine. Greet Asyncritus, Phlegon, Hermes, Patrobas, Hermas and the brethren with them. Greet Philologus and Julia, Nereus and his sister, and Olympas, and all the saints who are with them. Greet one another with a holy kiss. All the churches of Christ greet you.
>
> Now I urge you, brethren, keep your eye on those who cause dissensions and hindrances contrary to the teaching which you learned, and turn away from them. For such men are slaves, not of our Lord Christ but of their own appetites; and by their smooth and flattering speech they deceive the hearts of the unsuspecting. For the report of your obedience has reached to all; therefore I am rejoicing over you, but I want you to be wise in what is good and

innocent in what is evil. The God of peace will soon crush Satan under your feet. The grace of our Lord Jesus be with you.

Luke closed the holy book and said, "The Word of the Lord."

All the people responded, "Thanks be to God," and Luke left the pulpit.

Nora was so deeply comforted and affirmed that she just sat there enjoying being part of a community in which she belonged.

Cormac walked to the center in front of the altar, raised his Bible and said, "The Holy Gospel of our Lord Jesus Christ according to Matthew." Nora was confused yet again.

All the people rose and said, "Glory to you, Lord Christ."

Cormac began the twenty-eighth chapter:

> Now after the Sabbath, as it began to dawn toward the first day of the week, Mary Magdalene and the other Mary came to look at the grave. And behold, a severe earthquake had occurred, for an angel of the Lord descended from heaven and came and rolled away the stone and sat upon it. And his appearance was like lightning, and his clothing as white as snow. The guards shook for fear of him and became like dead men. The angel said to the women, "Do not be afraid; for I know that you are looking for Jesus who has been crucified. He is not here, for He has risen, just as He said. Come, see the place where He was lying. Go quickly and tell His disciples that He has risen from the dead; and behold, He is going ahead of you into Galilee, there you will see Him; behold, I have told you."
>
> And they left the tomb quickly with fear and great joy and ran to report it to His disciples. And behold, Jesus met them and greeted them. And they came up and took hold of His feet and worshiped Him. Then Jesus said to them, "Do not be afraid; go and take word to My brethren to leave for Galilee, and there they will see Me."

Cormac said, "The Gospel of the Lord."

All the people responded, "Praise to you, Lord Christ." Then they all sat down for the sermon.

Cormac simply prayed, "May the words of my mouth and the meditations of our hearts be acceptable in Your sight, O Lord our Rock and our Redeemer." He then began a preface to the sermon.

"Those of you who have made King of Kings your home church no doubt noticed that I very uncharacteristically veered from the lectionary this morning. The reason for the deviance was prompted by a meeting of the pastor's association I attended Tuesday morning. At that meeting I was extremely disappointed with our discussion of women's leadership in home and church. After years of Bible study, prayer, consultation with our deacons and our bishop, I wish to make our position perfectly clear. This morning I wish to preach on a few passages that give basic biblical support for that position.

"I will consciously avoid the usual labels because I realized this week how unhelpful they have become. One example is the word 'complementary.' Every one of my brothers at the meeting, who all have a high view of the Scriptures, and even those whose churches are on opposite ends of gender spectrum, claim to believe in gender complementarity. Nobody believes men and women are exactly the same. All agree that gender difference is created good by God. But for some gender difference is a reason for necessary inclusion according to gifts; others use it to exclude women from leadership. Some use it to define the genders by arguments from nature; others say we should be silent where the Bible is silent and see great harm to individuals in definitions of 'masculinity' and 'femininity.' Some say gender complementarity supports a hierarchy based on gender; others say it deconstructs it. The deacons and I, with support from the bishop, have agreed on the following statements. I will preach on them when they are relevant to the appropriate lectionary passages. I will read them as the language has been carefully chosen. The deacons tell us that these criteria would be followed in helping choose a new pastor if I were called elsewhere.

1. Leadership at King of Kings will be based on prayerful consideration of gifts, biblical qualifications, and individual circumstances, regardless of gender, race, ethnicity, or socioeconomic status.

2. We see the body rather than a ladder as the appropriate metaphor of organization in our community. Efficiency shall be promoted by individual connection to Christ our head. Everyone, and especially leaders, shall be encouraged to see themselves as bearing responsibilities and enjoying opportunities for service, not as playing roles.

3. Our attitude toward a husband and wife's relationship in the family shall be summarized by 'Submit to one another out of reverence for Christ.'

4. We refuse to define masculinity and femininity beyond clear biblical teaching. We will not pressure anyone to be more masculine or feminine. We will encourage people to be thankful for and content with their biological sex.

5. We see monogamous, heterosexual marriage and celibate singleness as equally high callings.

"This morning I certainly cannot do justice to all these ideas, but I can lay a foundation.

"One cannot overstate the importance of the second chapter of Genesis in both knowing and imagining how the world ought to be. In this short passage we are given our only narrative of human life before the fall. Everything after that lapse, even the inerrant Word, is set in a fallen world. All divine prescription from Genesis three onwards comes in the context of true description. And any true description from the moment of rebellion contains the reality of good perverted. 'How things are' became quite tangled up with and separated from 'How things ought to be.' But Moses and his later editors, inspired by the breath of the Spirit, speak with crystal clarity in this passage.

"Having just heard the history of creation, we hear how our first parents related to God and all of creation, and how we ought to relate to God and creation. The principle of rest is established, and then we get a focused second take on the creation of human beings. The man is placed in a garden of remarkable geographical detail, setting the story in and relating it to the ancient Near East. In the garden, man is to work and care for creation. He is given dominion over this vast and fruitful paradise and invited to freely use and enjoy it. One limit only, in the midst of perfect abundance, restricts him from the fruit of a single tree. God clarifies, warns and explains this prohibition to Adam directly, before the creation of Eve. Adam clearly bears responsibility for his maintenance of the prohibition before Eve is even created.

"While everything was yet flawless, creation was not complete or good until the creation of the woman. Adam was a finite creature with a lack. His primary relationship was with God. That relationship came first and empowered Adam for a secondary, a horizontal relationship. But, alas, nobody was there on his level. His relationship with God was vertical, with Adam at the bottom. His relationship with the rest of creation was vertical with him at the top. What he needed was another person who was like himself, not exactly like, for there must be a diversity of persons, but a person who shared his essential humanity, a person with whom he could stand side-by-side in the great scale of being. As has often been noted, the word for 'helper' does not imply subordination but a weakness in the one needing help. It is most often used in Scripture of God himself. Most often

Chapter 22

man needs help from God who is his helper (see for example, Psalm 54:4), not his lackey.

"With the rest of the created order, Adam was in contrast. What he wanted was a someone who was comparable, that is primarily like himself. He needed neither another god nor another subject. Just as the Godhead existed as a coequal diversity within unity, so human beings would bear the image of God in relationships of diversity within unity. Indeed, the very purpose of gender difference was unity. Creation was perfect and capable of fruitfulness when human beings could relate to one another in intimate unity.

"Adam yearned for a companion, and God saw that he needed a helper. God supplied both for his benefit. In Eve, Adam received a fellow creature that corresponded to him, who was like him, who shared his characteristics in his essential creaturehood. She was his speciesmate. She was 'according to his kind' just as the animals came in pairs according to their kinds. The word usually translated 'suitable' in 2:18 'emphasizes equality, for it means "face to face."'[3] His life became a shared experience with someone who could relate to him at his level. She was different enough to interest him and provide what he lacked, but what made him happy was that she was like him.

"Adam's first response to the creation of Eve is a paradigm for all human relationships. I ought to enter into any relationship joyously because this other person is essentially like me. Our basic equality then turns our differences from threat to enrichment. It is at this point, the important beginning point, that pipergrudemism departs from biblical mandate. It approaches the relationship through natural difference to arrive at equality, and thus never gets there. If a Gentile approaches a Jew saying, 'Jews are better money managers than Gentiles; therefore, Jews should always and forever, whether they want to or not, take the role of bankers; therefore, they are equal.' We say his premises deconstruct his conclusion, and we ought to consider our Gentile anti-Semitic. If a white person says of black people, 'They are better laborers, so "they" should serve in menial roles although they are equal.' The white person is simply racist; his very dependence upon stereotypical conclusions proves that he or she uses uncritical 'natural' arguments to justify permanent, involuntary separation of function based on racial difference, a class. It is the business of Christianity to reject dehumanizing claims of difference, to endeavor 'to keep the unity in the bond of peace,' and thus allow for the full expression of diversity

---

3. Nicole, "Biblical Egalitarianism and the Inerrancy of Scripture," 4–9.

according to gifts and callings.[4] The church is to recognize and utilize gifts and callings that God sovereignly gives, not to depend upon what seems natural to us.

"Both in the Bible and in history, God seems to delight in surprising us with his bestowal of gifts. In an age of slavery based on race, God gave gifts of scholarship and rhetoric to unschooled blacks, like Frederick Douglass and Olaudah Equiano. In a culture in which women were not allowed to testify in court because of their supposed inability to be truthful, God gives women the most unbelievable story to tell, and then scolds the men for not believing it.[5] He made women the apostles to the Apostles. He gave Hitler Jewish blood and Cherokees a gift for civilization. He brought the greatest king into the world in poverty. Based on a geographical stereotype, Nathanael asks the most foolish question of all, 'Can anything good can come out of Nazareth?'

"The most important places for the use of gifts and callings are within the church and family. And nowhere in Scripture are gifts and callings restricted to a certain class of people. These two communities are to be the primary focus of gifts and callings, the communities ordained by God which most edify people, and in which our service and relationships are our most intimate. But these are precisely the only communities in which hierarchicalists restrict women from service.

"I know a woman with an obvious gift for administration. She is the CEO of a large multinational corporation which she runs as though it is second nature. When a man in her church proposed marriage to her, she declined with the advice of her elders. They confirmed her gift and supported her choice for chaste singleness. When that same, large evangelical church was having a serious financial crisis, she was not allowed to help because she would have been 'doing the work of an ordained man.' This woman's profound isolation is decidedly unbiblical. She had neither nuclear family nor church in which to serve according to her gifts. But what about the damage that church did to its corporate self? Claiming a high view of the Scriptures, it denied service from a woman which was given by women in both Old and New Testaments and the early church. And a local body which had been salt and light dissolved. Now the leadership, of course, thought they were obeying biblical principle. And they are right that obedience does not always fit into the small box of human good sense.

4. See Ephesians 4:1–16.
5. See Luke 24:1–25.

Chapter 22

But it sounds much more like the principle of the eye saying to the hand, 'I have no need of you.' And the body fell apart, a victory for Satan and a grief for our Lord.

"Adam's response to Eve is quite different. It is his first and only recorded statement prior to the fall. It is also great poetry overflowing from a purely innocent emotion and attitude. When Adam says, 'This is bone of my bones / And flesh of my flesh; / She shall be called Woman, / Because she was taken out of Man,' he is overjoyed because she is like him (2:23). The poem may be paraphrased something like: This is wonderful; finally, a creature that is 'made of the same stuff' as I am.

"We may presume Adam was made earlier with sexual organs in anticipation of Eve, and that her biological differences were immediately apparent and attractive, but the poem is a celebration of their common humanity. The poem vents uncontainable joy over their kinship and comparability. Adam compares Eve to himself; that is he identifies ways in which they are alike. It is not a statement of contrast, he does not tell ways in which they are different. Most certainly there are differences, and those differences are good. But Adam is excited here about her kinship to him.

"Genesis 2:1-3 summarizes the first, the bird's eye narrative of creation by emphasizing the successful completion of creation. The creator brought everything into existence in perfect accordance with his will. Upon that principle the Sabbath is established. To desist from work concludes a cycle of labor and rest, a pattern, a healthy rhythm of life that, even after the fall, is prescriptive.

"Genesis 2:4-6 prologues a closer narrative of Adam and Eve's creation. We are given a more detailed narrative. Sequence and substance of creation are important elements for proper interpretation. The male is created first and from dust. He is placed in a paradise and called to reflect his likeness to God and his superior mental capacity by classifying and naming the species of animals. The 'male and female' phrase from the first chapter establishes that Adam was created with sexual organs that anticipate the creation of Eve.

"Verses 10-14 situate Eden in a precise geographical location that establishes a literary context for the narrative. Genesis is provided to an original audience in the ancient Near East, and it shares particular literary elements and generic conventions with pagan myths and epics. Literary similarities contrast the God of the Hebrews to the pagan gods. Similar literary elements emphasize the different points of the narratives. If we assume Moses as author in the fifteenth century BC, he writes to an audience already familiar with myths such as *The Descent of Inanna*, *Enuma Elish*, and *The Epic of Gilgamesh*. And God's creation story is clarified by seeing it in contrast to men's creation stories. For this is the creation narrative among creation narratives, and one that challenges all the others.

"Gender difference is the only difference explicitly addressed in Genesis 2, for gender difference is the deepest difference in humanity. If we see 'how it ought to be' there, before the fall, with the most essential difference in humanity, we can get it right anywhere. Racial, cultural and class differences can influence us deeply, but those influences are social constructs. Race, for example is only skin deep until our environment molds us according to our race.

"Zora Neale Hurston eloquently shows how the influence of racial difference changes according to situation, but at the core of her personality she is 'the eternal feminine with its string of beads.'[6] In many Western cultures lighter skin is related to social prestige. But in the Luo culture of East Africa, children whose skin is not the purest black are mocked as 'tomatoes.' Paul ignores race in the escalating scale of diversity in Galatians 3:28, not because it is outside his point, but because it can be presupposed within it.

"Diversity of culture, socioeconomic class, and gender should be embraced, only sin should be rejected. Patriarchy is sin. In the church of Jesus Christ separation by class is the taboo. Equality of being and deep unity are to be respected; preferential status denied."

The priest sat down, as he always did, and provided a few moments of pure silence. The congregation sat and allowed for intellectual digestion and the Spirit's work. Then Cormac said, "Let us summarize the content of our faith using the Nicene Creed.

> We believe in one God, the Father, the Almighty, maker of heaven and earth, of all that is, seen and unseen.
> We believe in one Lord, Jesus Christ, the only Son of God, eternally begotten of the Father, God from God, Light from Light, true God from true God, begotten, not made, of one Being with the Father. Through him all things were made. For us and for our salvation he came down from heaven: by the power of the Holy Spirit he became incarnate from the Virgin Mary, and was made man. For our sake he was crucified under Pontius Pilate; he suffered death and was buried. On the third day he rose again in accordance with the Scriptures; he ascended into heaven and is seated at the right

---

6. Hurston, "How It Feels To Be Colored Me."

Chapter 22

hand of the Father. He will come again in glory to judge the living and the dead, and his kingdom will have no end.

We believe in the Holy Spirit, the Lord, the giver of life, who proceeds from the Father and the Son. With the Father and the Son he is worshiped and glorified. He has spoken through the Prophets.

We believe in one holy catholic and apostolic Church.

We acknowledge one baptism for the forgiveness of sins.

We look for the resurrection of the dead, and the life of the world to come. Amen."

Then Cormac prayed, "Gracious Father, we pray for thy holy catholic church. Fill it with all truth, in all truth with all peace. Where it is corrupt, purify it; where it is in error, direct it; where in anything it is amiss, reform it. Where it is right, strengthen it; where it is in want, provide for it; where it is divided, reunite it; for the sake of Jesus Christ thy Son our Savior. *Amen.*"

A short pause ensued before the people began their spontaneous and passionate praises, petitions, and thanksgivings. They prayed for one another, current events, and whatever God put upon their hearts. Six-year-old Billy Kiser prayed for his dog, Wally, who "had tons of fleas."

After the Eucharist, Cormac said, "I would like to close our service today as I would a truly 'traditional' wedding. I borrow traditional prayer book language. It does not describe that role-playing monster that didn't appear until the early 1970s, but a beautiful relationship rooted in the perfection of Genesis 2. The curse challenged that beauty by perverting both men's and women's natures with a desire for control. May we work to redeem marriages, and especially our own, with a passion for freedom through loving service. This is a prayer that never once defines masculinity and femininity—because the Bible does not. It does not elevate the married life above, nor devalue it under, the single life. It emphasizes love and mutual submission to one another out of reverence for Christ. It asks of God a marriage which meets the needs of all people, and it describes a marriage which is attractive to our young people. In it one sees the unity that can come of diversity and how our loving God has established monogamous, heterosexual marriage as the basis of Christian society."

He prayed, "Eternal God, creator and preserver of all life, author of salvation, and giver of all grace: Look with favor upon the world you have made, and for which your Son gave his life, and especially upon men and women whom you make one flesh in Holy Matrimony.

"Give us wisdom and devotion in the ordering of their common life, that each may be to the other a strength in need, a counselor in perplexity, a comfort in sorrow, and a companion in joy.

"Grant that our wills may be so knit together in your Will, and our spirits in your Spirit, that we may grow in love and peace with you and one another all the days of our life.

"Give us grace, when we hurt each other, to recognize and acknowledge our fault, and to seek each other's forgiveness and yours.

"Make our life together a sign of Christ's love to this sinful and broken world, that unity may overcome estrangement, forgiveness heal guilt, and joy conquer despair.

"Bestow on us, if it is your will, the gift and heritage of children, and the grace to bring them up to know you, to love you, and to serve you.

"Give us such fulfillment of our mutual affection that we may reach out in love and concern for others.

"Grant that all married persons who have witnessed these vows may find their lives strengthened and their loyalties confirmed.

"Grant that the bonds of our common humanity, by which all your children are united one to another, and the living to the dead, may be so transformed by your grace, that your Will may be done on earth as it is in heaven; where, O Father, with your Son, and the Holy Spirit, you live and reign in perfect unity, now and for ever. *Amen.*

"Now, go in peace to love and serve the Lord."

When Nora rose, turned, and reached for her coat, she saw Jill and Ted only two rows behind her. They were looking deeply into one another's eyes and smiling two very joyful smiles. Next to Jill sat Tom and Hannah Mullins, and next to Ted sat Shane Sayers.

Chapter 23

Do not forsake your own friend ...
Better *is* a neighbor nearby than a brother far away.

—Proverbs 27:10

At 11:50 on Friday, May 9, Jill threw her shoulders back and pressed the palms of her hands down on her lower back as she waddled toward the student union. Ted was "taking her out to lunch," which meant in their relational jargon that he had made two of his super peanut butter sandwiches. Jill would stop at Cascades and use the last dollars on her BlueridgeCard for two fresh-squeezed orange juices and frozen strawberry smoothies, and then meet Ted upstairs in the Profile Trail Lounge at a table for two.

This was the last day of finals week, and Ted and Jill had both had a nine-to-nooner. Jill felt a huge relief to be entirely finished for the semester. Holly would begin her anatomy exam at noon, and Jill prayed for her as she painfully made her way along. Campus was almost deserted. Most students had taken their last exam, finished packing, and gone home. Megan's last exam had been Wednesday, and Dr. Clery had driven up from Concord and loaded Megan's stuff, and most of Holly and Jill's, in his pickup and taken Megan home. Jill's mother would arrive around six o'clock this evening to take Holly, Jill, and the rest of their things home for the summer and the birth.

Jill had such mixed feelings about going home. She was eager to be with her family, and almost anxious to be near Dr. and Mrs. Billingham and their hospital with its cozy birthing center wing. She had carefully thought through her birth plan and visited the birthing center during spring break. It would be so great to be with caregivers she knew and trusted. She wanted so much to have a drugless, natural birth, and she knew they would not medically intervene unless it was truly necessary. Holly and Jill's mom would coach her. Holly had even gone to childbirth classes with her. It felt right to be going home, but for Ted.

He had recently been accepted to Regent's Park College, Oxford. His Michaelmas term did not begin until late September, so she'd see him for about a month after she returned to Poplar in August . . . with a baby. Jill was very grateful for his opportunity of a lifetime, but she hated to part from him.

Darren and Katie had been up in March to visit their sisters, and Jill had been delighted at how well they had liked Ted. He had taken them all zip-lining on Mullins Mountain that Saturday. It had been a fantastic afternoon. Jill's big belly had prevented her full participation, but it had been all the more fun to watch the others. It had been so important to Jill that they would enjoy and respect each other, but she need not have worried. Darren and Katie were predisposed to respect him for befriending Jill in her condition. Darren had even invited Ted to stay with him at the Billingham's for a few days after the birth. Ted could tell that Darren thought deeply about ideas and was committed to serving people.

After getting the smoothies Jill headed up the stairs. With a smoothie in each hand, she could neither grab the hand rail nor support her lower back with her hands. The painful and arduous trek to the second floor took almost five minutes. "Today I should have taken the elevator," she thought. When she arrived at last in the lounge, Ted was already waiting for her. His usual smile faded when he saw her.

"You look awful," he said with concern.

"Oh, thanks—Just what a girl likes to hear," she said with a grin in spite of that horrible backache.

"No really," he asked, "how do you feel?"

"I've felt rotten for the last two days," she answered. Ted noted that this was the first time Jill had complained to him about how the pregnancy was making her feel.

"When was the last time you saw the midwife?" he asked as he switched the sandwiches to a lower table next to an easy chair and relieved Jill of the smoothies.

Jill replied, "I saw her on Wednesday morning. She said everything looked fine. She estimated that the baby is about seven pounds and head down. She said I wasn't dilated or effaced. I felt great then, but that evening I had cramps and spent most of the evening in the bathroom. Then I got a backache. It kept me from sleeping Wednesday night, and it was almost

Chapter 23

impossible to study for my cultural geography final on Thursday. I made it through my final this morning, but barely. This backache is killing me."

Ted helped her into the soft upholstered chair and prayed for her back and gave thanks for their food. He handed her a sandwich and set the smoothie on the table next to her.

He said, "When my mom was pregnant with Sammy, she had backaches. She would always get down on all fours and arch her back like a cat. Do you ever do that?"

"Yeah," she said. "That's how I studied on Thursday. I put my geography notes on the floor and got down on all fours. I spent most of the day like that. But I couldn't very well do that in class. It was excruciating by the time I finished."

Ted got up and looked around the corner. "Why don't you do it now? Nobody's here but us. I'll keep watch and warn you if somebody comes."

Jill responded with, "Oh, thanks Ted, that would be a relief!" and awkwardly got down on all fours. With her knees under her hips and her hands on the floor under her shoulders, she slowly arched her back and tucked her chin while he munched at his sandwich and kept a lookout. Then she swayed her back and lifted her head, just as her childbirth instructor had taught her. She did this several times, and suddenly exclaimed, "Ted, the baby just moved more than I've ever felt! I think he or she completely flipped over! My backache is gone!"

"Fantastic!" he said. "Let me help you up." He placed his right arm across her back and grabbed just below her right shoulder. His left hand firmly held her near shoulder and lifted. Following a genuine effort on both their parts, Jill gained her feet.

"That was really amazing—instant relief. Thanks so much. I am such a beached whale," she exclaimed with embarrassment.

"I doubt I'd be doing any better with an extra thirty pounds off the front," he consoled . . . He saw her jaw suddenly drop and her face flush crimson. "What's the matter?"

He followed her gaze to the tile floor to see her standing in a puddle. Then he glanced up her legs. Her jeans were soaked all the way up the inside. "Wow," he whispered, "looks like your water broke." Speechless, she just nodded, standing like an inanimate pillar. Through Ted's mind flashed a pillar of salt that was Lott's wife.

"Maybe you should call your midwife? I've got my mom's car. I could drive you if she wants to see you," he suggested. Again the pillar with the red

149

face at the top nodded. He grabbed her backpack from the chair next to the waiting smoothies and untasted sandwich. She pulled her phone out of the small side pocket, and began scrolling down her contacts when the pillar of salt began to crumble like a sandcastle caught by a wave. The red at the top had turned white. She dropped her phone, and Ted reached to support her. He guided her to the chair, and she sat out on the edge of the seat with her knees rather apart supporting her hands. Her eyes were closed, and she was focusing on breathing deeply. Ted knew she was having a strong contraction, and he looked at his watch. He noted 12:17, hoping another strong one wouldn't come before 12:27. He remembered something about "less than ten minutes apart." The contraction lasted longer than he thought it should. In the meanwhile he plucked the unharmed phone off the floor. When he saw her relax, he handed her the phone. He watched her slow down in the N's and tap "Nurse-midwife."

The ringing seemed to last forever. Finally somebody picked up and said, "This is Sanora. How are you Jill?"

"My water broke, and I just had a whopper of a contraction," Jill answered laconically.

"Is somebody with you who can drive you to our office? I'd like to check you," Sanora said.

Jill looked pleadingly at Ted. He nodded with a smile. Jill said, "Yes."

"Good, I'll see you as soon as you can safely get here. No need to rush," Sanora cautioned.

Jill reached for her backpack and slipped the phone into its pocket. Ted rewrapped the sandwiches in a flash and stuffed them in his backpack. As Jill slipped her backpack onto her shoulders, Ted grabbed the smoothies; and they headed toward the elevator. Ted thought the elevator took forever to open. As they arrived at the ground floor, he heard Jill gasp and saw her face again turn that ugly white.

"Just breathe," he said far more calmly than he felt. He glanced at his watch and thought, "Oh shoot! Just less than five minutes." The doors started to close; Ted stepped into the doorway, but saw Jill lean forward. He let the doors close and went to Jill. He stood directly in front of her, and she rested on his back through the rest of the contraction. When it had passed, he pressed the button and the doors opened on the ground floor.

They walked around the Crossroads Coffeehouse and down the long hall that had flags from every country supplying a BRSU student—so many. They threaded their way through the empty bookstore and up the sidewalk

Chapter 23

to the parking structure. Ted shot up a prayer of thanks that he had found a ground-floor parking space that morning. Even so, she began another contraction as he was opening the door for her. He checked his watch. "Drat! Less than five minutes again," he anxiously estimated.

After the contraction she didn't get right into the passenger seat, but said, "I don't want to get your mom's car seat damp."

He felt like yelling, "So what!" Instead, he opened the back door and snatched up Sammy's old sweatshirt that he had left lying on the seat. He spread it out on the passenger seat. And Jill got in and buckled up.

By the time Ted had come around to the driver's side, Jill had her phone out. She tapped a number, and after only one ring her mother's voice massage came on. After the tone Jill said to the device, "Hi, Mom. This is Jill. I'm in labor. Please call me as soon as you can." By the time Ted had rounded the AppalCart circle and started down Howard Street, Jill had put in another call. Again, a quick transfer to voicemail, and Jill said, "Hey, Holly, I'm in labor. Ted's driving me to the midwife's. I guess you won't get this message until after your final, but please call ASAP."

Ted turned right on the 321. When they stopped at a red light at the Convocation Center, Jill started another hard contraction. Ted's watch told him the alarming news—four and a half minutes, even a little closer together. This time it was Ted who made a call. His dad picked up and cheerfully said, "Hi, Theo. What's up?" The tone of Theo's answer told him that something was definitely up.

"Dad, I need help. Jill's contractions are four and a half minutes apart. Her mom is more than two hours away and hasn't even gotten her message. Her friend Holly is taking a final exam with her phone off. I'm driving her to the midwife's," tensely tumbled out.

James Mullins took a deep breath before calmly, but strongly saying, "Sounds like you do need help, and you know how to get it and from whom. Jill needs you to stay with her until she asks you to leave. She needs you to think clearly because she may not be able to for a while. She needs your support and encouragement. As soon as your mother gets back from Alison's violin lesson in Sugar Grove, we'll drive in to the hospital to see how you are doing. I'll be praying for you both. See you later."

The light turned green, and Ted said, "Gotta go, thanks, Dad."

It seemed to Ted that Jill was slipping into another world. He didn't want to bother her, but he asked, "Is Sanora's office across the street from the Watauga Medical Center on Deerfield?"

"Yes, just around the corner on Doctor's Drive—right next to OrthoCarolina," she said.

They breezed through the intersection at the 105 on a green light, and so Jill didn't start another contraction until they turned into the parking lot. Ted saw a sign that read "Watauga Obstetrics and Gynecology." He parked in front of the door and went around to help her out. After the contraction ended, she got out and they entered the office.

Sanora was waiting for them. She took them into an examination room and had Jill lie down on a padded table. She motioned Ted into a chair in the corner and then pulled a curtain around three sides of Jill on the padded table. He heard a zipper and some shifting sounds then the snap of a latex glove. In a few moments Sanora asked, "Didn't I just see you Wednesday? How have you been feeling since then?"

Jill began, "Wednesday evening I felt rotten, and I had very bad diarrhea. After that I had a horrible backache until . . ." But she couldn't finish because Ted could tell she was having another contraction. He prayed for her and himself; he did know where their help came from.

A few minutes later Ted heard Sanora say, "Well that backache did a lot of work. You are completely effaced and five centimeters dilated. I want you checked in across the street right away."

Jill started to cry and said, "No, I can't. I'm planning to have the baby in Charlotte. My mom and Holly are going to be with me. Dr. and Mrs. Billingham will be my medical caregivers."

Sanora said, "I'm afraid this baby has changed your plans. You are too far along to go farther than across the street. It's possible you wouldn't make it as far as Hickory. Things are more likely to speed up than slow down." Ted just heard Jill crying.

He stood up and walked around the curtain. He went up next to her ear and in a strong whisper said, "We can do this together. I'll stay with you. I may not know what to do except love you through it, but I want to do that. Please let me serve you in this way."

Through her tears she said, "Oh, Ted, you're so kind, but it's not your responsibility. You don't have to do this."

He kissed her beautiful Mahogany hair for the first time and said, "I want to share this responsibility with you. I know that I don't have to, but I want to do this. It isn't safe for you to drive to Charlotte now."

She asked, "You won't leave me?"

"No way," he said and kissed her again.

Chapter 23

Jill looked down at Sanora and said, "If Ted can stay with me, I'll go across the street."

Sanora smiled and said, "Let's get going. Ted, would you bring me that wheelchair, please?"

Chapter 24

So God created man in his own image, in the image of God created he him; male and female created he them.

—Genesis 1: 27

These past months Ted had been increasingly critical of the concept of "role." Indeed, he could not remember reading support for gender roles outside of clearly sexist texts. But the moment they arrived at the birthing center, he found himself in a position rooted in biological sexuality, a role (perhaps) looking different in different cultures, but, nevertheless, with universal elements. He was living out the father, although he was not the father, because he was male. Jill was female, so she could and was doing things that he could never do. He was doing things she could not do.

She was having a contraction when they arrived at the admissions desk, so Ted gave the clerk her information. Ted gave physical, spiritual, and emotional support while Jill was utterly controlled by her female bodily functions. He lifted her back when she couldn't. He prayed when she couldn't. He made decisions when she couldn't. When Sanora was out of the room, at about nine centimeters, an LVN saw Jill's intense pain and suggested an epidural. Ted saw longing for relief in Jill's eyes. But he thought about what Jill really wanted. He knew that Sanora thought things were progressing well. The last thing she had cheerfully said before leaving the room was that "Jill's contractions are very productive." He also knew the baby's heart rate was responding normally to Jill's contractions, so he said with a conviction and clarity that he did not feel, "She doesn't want that!" Jill's response was to squeeze his hand in support of him and smile the briefest of fleeting smiles through her blood-shot eyes.

Ted's image of Jill during the entire ordeal was one of her overwhelming power. Her body became miraculous in his mind. It knew what to do far beyond consciousness. God worked his power to bring forth life through

Chapter 24

this beautiful and mysterious body. He wondered what it would be like to possess such a powerful body, and he yet he knew he was glad he would never endure that sort of pain. He appreciated Jill as a woman as only a man can.

Ted never forgot the moment when Jill went from a very passive strength to an all-consuming activity. When they had settled into their room in the birthing center, Sanora had checked Jill again and said, "Excellent, already seven." The comment had dredged up from Ted's memory something his dad had said right after Sammy's birth. He had come out of their room leaving his mother in the care of the midwife to tell them that they had a healthy, new brother. Then he had said to Ted, "Theo, if you ever get married and have a family, remember this; it is a sin to remember anything your wife says between seven and ten centimeters dilation." At the time Ted thought the comment really off-the-wall, but when he saw Jill at that time, he understood. She was trying to not get in the way of her own body. In spite of the intensity, she could do nothing actively to help. Her job was utter passivity in the face of her own bodily power. Relief of any sort became the great impossibility. Herculean contractions lasted longer than the time between them. It seemed the longest forty-five minutes in his life. And then everything changed in the blink of an eye when Jill simply said, "Push."

Immediately Sanora's latexed hand examined for the last time, and she gleefully said to Jill, "Yes, you're ten. Now push through the contractions." And Jill's job changed. She now became the active supporter of her body, and she consciously augmented her contractions.

Until that time Ted had little to do with what happened below Jill's waist. The few times he glanced that direction, he saw only the light blanket covering her hip and either her back or her basketball. His focus had been her north end. He spoke encouragement into her ear, he held her hand, he fed her ice chips, he brushed her damp hair out of her face. But after the ten centimeter pronouncement, Sanora slipped sterile sheets under Jill's body, and she now preferred to lay on her back with pillows raising her to what Ted thought of as a crunch position. When they had entered the room, Ted had relaxed when he saw that it looked much like a regular bedroom with a regular queen-sized bed. He now noticed that the footboard supported Jill's feet particularly well.

During pushing contractions Ted provided more support to her arched back until he thought his own back would break. He amazed himself when he kicked off his shoes, got up on the bed with Jill, put his back against the headboard, and supported her back with his shins. Jill, who was now seeming much more like herself, even smiled and said, "Thanks!"

Even in the midst of this physical intimacy, Ted was conscious of giving Jill her privacy. From his perch at the headboard, he could see her spread knees and her feet against the footboard, but he was glad the sterile-sheeted basketball prevented his vision of areas of her body that he had not earned access to through a mutual, lifelong commitment.

In spite of this awareness, his interest was now becoming divided between supporting Jill from the north and the infant's progress. He became very curious now about all activity in the south. By the time the assistant midwife had opened, what Ted had thought was an armoire, to reveal an incubated, transparent bassinet and a bunch of stainless steel hospital-looking equipment, he had forgotten about Jill's needs. The last minutes of pushing, Ted was still physically supporting Jill, but they were together consumed entirely with the anticipation of the moment when this child would enter the world. They could not see the crowning. Their togetherness mutually focused away from one another and fused in concern for the child. Between the last two contractions, Ted whispered into Jill's ear, "Dear Father, please bring this baby safely to us." Then their world blossomed.

Ted could see, even through the sterile sheet, the basketball squeezing out of shape from an extraordinary contraction. With a deep orgasmic sigh and push from Jill, a baby smoothly glided into Sanora's waiting hands. The midwife gently stroked the baby's nose downward, and the child let out a lusty howl. Jill immediately reached for the baby, seeing him indistinctly through tears of joy. Ted's vision was better, but he also cried for joy. They watched the baby's color change as though by magic.

When Sanora reached for the sterile sheet on the deflated basketball, Ted turned away remembering her privacy and looked to Jill's radiant face. He felt he saw her soul in that beautiful vision. She was sweaty, disheveled, and exhausted. In outward beauty, she was at her worst. But her whole soul reached out in love for her child. Ted suddenly felt like the great outsider, with no right to be part of this exquisite embrace. This was not his son. Jill was not his wife. His tears of joy became tears of devastation; he wept for grief.

Jill heard the change, and even as Sanora laid her newborn son on her belly for the first time, she hugged the child to her body with her left hand, and drew Ted into her with her right. His cheek snugged up to her

Chapter 24

shoulder; his left hand combed into her hair, and his right hand caressed the little boy. This gendered circle of love redeemed this evidence of the fall. What some sexist men meant for evil, God meant for good.

The warmth flowing into Ted's cheek from Jill's shoulder radiated throughout his body augmenting his power to love a hundredfold. That power of love transferred to the boy from his own hand. The baby touching and needing Jill stimulated her power to love well beyond herself. None of them originated this love. Love is from God, and he bestows that love most clearly in these, first human then gendered, relationships. The most fruitful of all loves flowed in relational trinity.

Suddenly the youngest member of this trinity sent up another howl. Jill looked at Sanora and asked, "Can I? Is it OK now?"

Sanora smilingly answered, "It will help deliver the placenta."

Ted didn't know what they were talking about. Jill's right hand left his shoulder and slid down to the baby under the sheets so that she was holding him firmly around his chest with both her hands. She looked at Ted with warm and patient tenderness and asked, "Ted, will you please pull the sheet down so I can try to nurse the baby?" He nodded with shyness and alarm, but didn't seem able to move. She added, "It's OK, you can stay with us." He was by that empowered to reveal her breasts.

He watched the most beautiful event he had ever seen from a vantage point within the circle of love. Her breasts were gorgeous. They were not objects she owned, but an important part of the wholeness of her personhood. With them she offered comfort and nourishment to her child, and he hoped now, more than ever before, that one day he might caress her there. She laid the baby down between her breasts as she scooted into a more upright position. Ted helped her. She then cradled the little guy in the crook of her left arm. She held her breast with her right hand between her pointing and her middle finger where the honey-oak colored curve met the walnut colored circle. She raised the child to her and gently brushed the tip of the nipple against his cheek. Instantly, his mouth flew open, but his howling ceased as he latched on and gobbled the walnut circle into his mouth. Tentatively at first and then with greedy abandon, he nursed away. Jill and Ted relaxed at the mesmerizing sight. It was one thing to bring a child into the world and quite another to feel you could take good care of him. The sight seemed a sign from God that he would use them to provide for the child.

It seemed then that Jill's labor began all over again. She had five hard contractions very close together. During the fifth, Ted heard a heavy, wet, plop. And Sanora exclaimed, "Great, the placenta is delivered whole. That little guy's vigorous nursing is your best prevention against hemorrhage; let him nurse away."

As the newborn seemed to know his duty and kept at it, Jill looked shyly at Ted. She hesitated, not quite knowing how to say what she felt she ought. Finally she said, "Ted, I really want to name him Theodore, but I don't want you to feel any obligation to us. You have been a wonderful friend to me through this, and I want to honor you by giving him your name. But I don't want you to think I'm trying to hook you into anything beyond friendship."

Ted thought for a few moments and then answered, "I am very honored that you want to name him Theodore, but I'd like you to think about it in a different way. I would like you to see his name as a promise to me that when I am able to properly care for you, you will consider marrying me. If I was finished with school and had a job, I would ask you today to marry me. I love you. I now love your baby, and I desperately wish we were a family. I am so thankful to have gone through this day with you; God seems to have shown me his and my own mind in this awesome experience. I don't think I'll ever feel close enough to you. I cannot now say when I'll be able to, but I want to marry you now. I feel absolutely no obligation, only passionate desire." And he kissed her for the very first time on her luscious lips.

Jill thought that perhaps this was the first time in her life, when she was actually aware of who she really was. She felt God loving her through Ted's love coming in through her lips. She felt God's love flowing out her breast to her son. She also knew she deeply loved Ted, and she knew her son would eventually love her. She thought of God loving her by sacrificing his son for them all. Somehow, that was who she was, the object and giver of love. She reached for Ted's hand and prayed, "Oh loving God, Please help us to never violate your love for us, or ours for one another. Thank you for giving us love."

They had long since forgotten anyone else was in the room. But now they heard a knock on the door, and Sanora went to open it. There stood a frantic Juanita Kelly. She looked toward the bed and burst out, "Oh Jilly, I came the second I got your message! Are you OK?"

Jill smiled broadly and said, "Mom, I've never been better in my life. Come over and meet your grandson. His name is Theodore Robert Kelly. And greet Ted, who stood in for you today with amazing style. He's been the best sort of rock."

Chapter 24

Mrs. Kelly went over to Ted, cupped his chin in her hands, looked almost fiercely into his eyes and said, "Thank you—You are a remarkable young man. God bless you." She looked down at the nursing baby, cupped his tiny head in her hand and cooed, "Oh my little Teddy, welcome to our family, and most welcome." Then she looked at Jill and said, "No mother could be more proud of a daughter than I am of you. Your faith and character have matured well beyond your nineteen years. Congratulations my daughter-mother."

Just then they heard another knock on the door, and in slipped Holly. "I'm so sorry to have missed it," she whined, "I so much wanted to be there for you, Jill. Are you well?"

"I had a wonderful support crew in Ted," replied Jill, "But maybe you can help out now. Sanora, this is my friend, Holly, who plans to become a midwife; Is there anything she can do to help you?"

"Well, Jill, how would you feel about Holly cutting the cord, and then helping me with the weighing and measuring?" asked Sanora. Holly's face beamed with anticipation.

Jill answered, "Excellent plan."

Then commenced a lecture by Sanora to Holly on placenta wholeness and assessing the amount of maternal bleeding. Holly was now in her element. When she cut the cord, she had accepted with humility the honor bestowed upon her.

By this time Teddy, as he had now several times been called, was running out of gas for nursing. And Ted suggested that this might be a good time to weigh and measure him. Jill agreed, but, nevertheless, found it very difficult to give him up. When she could bring herself to it, she lifted him into Ted's arms for the journey across the room. He accepted the great gift. Teddy accepted the change graciously and looked for several moments into Ted's face. Those gazes established a bond that survived the rest of their lives. Ted had scarce an easier time parting with Teddy than Jill, but he eventually laid him down in the warm bassinet for the official inspection.

The recorded verdicts were: Apgar score at one minute, 9. Apgar score at five minutes, a whopping 10. Weight, 7 pounds 9 ounces. Height, 20 inches. All these numbers helped to relax everyone except Teddy, who resumed howling until Ted returned him to his mother's breast. Sanora noted that he nursed equally well on her right side, and she mentioned it to Holly, who now had on her own latex gloves. Sanora then began to explain to Holly the superficiality of Jill's few perineal tears, why she would not do any repair, and why Sanora was confident they would heal quickly on their own. Ted was very glad to leave the care and cleanup of Jill's south to those two.

Juanita Kelly now entered their circle of love. Jill was still having occasional contractions, but they were so easy in comparison to those earlier that she welcomed them. For she knew that they were helping her uterus clamp down. When Teddy again exhausted himself with nursing, Sanora suggested that Ted hold him while she taught Holly how to massage Jill's fundus. Ted sat in the rocking chair next to Jill's bed looking into the face of the little one who he hoped would one day be his son. And Teddy looked up at him, seeming to imprint Ted's face into his inner being. Jill's right hand rested either on Ted's shoulder or the baby's head as she was cleaned up and worked on.

It suddenly occurred to Ted that perhaps he and Teddy were in a traditionally women's space. But he came to the conclusion that the idea was silly. Teddy's life depended on being loved by Jill, and Ted felt like this was where he belonged. First Corinthians 11:12 flashed through his mind and lent support to his belonging in this space and to his growing appreciation of mutuality. "For as woman came from man, so man comes from woman; but all things are from God." He thought, "Where's the hierarchy in that? Sounds egalitarian to me."

Teddy started to squirm, and Ted thought it was time to give him back to Jill. "This is real teamwork," he thought. But as he rose out of the chair, he felt a rumble inside the hand holding Teddy's bottom. The blanket instantly stained, and Ted found his hand full of a tarry, sticky, viscous stool. "Yuck," he said as some of the nasty stuff dropped onto his shirt. Everyone in the room but Teddy laughed at him. He smiled and handed him to Holly to clean up while he went to the sink on his own behalf.

Holly said, "This is great; now we know his plumbing works. It's meconium. Sanora, where are the diapers?"

Sanora answered, "Top drawer," as she opened the door to yet another tapping. A nurse whispered something to her.

"Ted," said Sanora, "all the way down the hall to the right is the maternity waiting room. Maybe you should go down, and see who's there."

Ted dried his hands and looked at Jill. She smiled and nodded, and Ted headed down the hall. A crowd of familiar faces met him in the waiting room. His mom and dad rushed toward him with hugs. He saw Dr. Shaw and her husband. Lydia and Mike were there, and so were Uncle Hank and Aunt Kathy. Ted announced to the concerned faces, "Everybody's fine. Jill

Chapter 24

was a trooper. It's a boy, seven pounds nine ounces, twenty inches long, great Apgar scores . . . And . . . Well . . . his name is Theodore. Everybody in there is calling him Teddy. He's terrific. Jill's recovering very well." He wanted to go on to say something about the more important part, about how the three of them loved one another . . . but he didn't know how to say it right. There was a long pause as though everyone knew there was more and were waiting for it.

Suddenly a red-haired, freckled fireball burst into the room with her green eyes flashing. "Did she have the baby? Are they OK? I came as soon as I heard she was in labor," spewed Megan.

Ted responded, "They're fine; I'll take you back to see them." To the original audience, he said, "I'll be right back."

He took Megan down to Jill and Teddy's room and let Jill give the details to Megan; then he asked her if she'd like to see Dr. Shaw and his parents. He returned to the waiting room and invited Dr. Shaw and his mother and father back to the room. They admired the baby and congratulated Jill, but didn't stay long, knowing Jill should rest and have privacy. Back in the waiting room, the Shaws, Aunt Kathy and Uncle Frank, Lydia and Mike all said good-bye and asked to be kept in touch. When they were gone, the three of them sat together on a sofa. James Mullins had his arm around his son. Magdalene Mullins asked him, "What about you, Theo? Where are you in this now?"

"So much has happened between us today, Mom. I feel like a different person than I was this morning." He turned to his father, "Dad you gave me some good advice. She really did need me to stay with her. When you told me to, I thought, 'She needs Holly, or her mother, she doesn't need me.' But she did, and I discovered that I needed her. Dad, Mom, I want them to be my family when I can take proper care of them. I love Jill and Teddy more than I can tell you."

"She's a wonderful woman, son. You're on a good path for becoming able to take care of them, but it will be a long and difficult time of preparation, feeling as you do so early in your education."

"I know, Dad, I hate the thought of leaving them. But look at what God has done for us already; can't I trust him to bring us together if he means for us to marry—even if it's several years."

"You can trust him for that—to be sure." They began praying with thanksgiving for new life, the miracle of birth, and God's love to them, so that they might enjoy abundant life. Then they prayed together for the future, pleading with God for clarity and guidance. They prayed for Jill's wisdom and strength as a single mother. They prayed for little Teddy to trust in Christ at an early age and to grow in love and grace and in favor with God and man. They prayed that they would not reduce their lives to what they could understand, but to trust God in the true mystery and complexity of reality. They prayed that God would lead Ted on a straight path toward financial independence, so that he might support his family well. But in this last Ted was not sure that he and his father agreed on what that meant.

Ted did not feel that he understood what it meant. He was absolutely certain it meant loving service with Christ as model, but he could never get very far beyond that. He wasn't sure he wanted to. He wanted to share life with Jill, not divide their lives into separate spheres. He wanted to work with her as a partner, not assume the role of sole supporter. He wanted to make a life together, rather than make a life for Jill and Teddy. He remembered the feeling of joy he felt when they were alone in their circle of love, each comforting and being comforted by the touch of the others. He wanted to relate, and he could not imagine how playing a gender role would not harm relationship, reduce knowledge of the individual, and deemphasize communication. Ted wanted to talk to Jill and Teddy, to understand what they were thinking and feeling and then to decide and act with an existential dependence on God and his Word.

In spite of the greyness of the last part of his dad's prayer, Ted was much comforted. He had never been more thankful that his parents were faithful people of godly character. He had never in his life needed to doubt their love for him. And they had never deconstructed his trust in God; indeed, they did all they could to promote it. They were sinful like all people, but they repented. Ted could remember many occasions when Mom or Dad had confessed being too harsh or too unconcerned, too lazy or too preoccupied with the trivial. They said things like, "In this particular situation I was unloving and selfish; please forgive me."

This last thought clarified his remaining question about Jill. Would she forgive him if he deeply hurt her? He had already sinned against her many times, but she didn't see it. He had repented quietly in prayer. But those experiences taught him that, however he may desire not to, he was fully capable of treating her badly. Would she really forgive, or would she withhold her love when he obviously did not deserve it? That was the only fear he knew he had of her. It would, he knew, take tremendous courage for him to repent of sinning against her. The thought of pleading for her

Chapter 24

forgiveness brought terror into his bones. And yet, he realized that was the only way he would really know whether she really loved him in the way he wanted to be loved. Ted wanted Jill to love him in spite of his culpability. And this was what he felt he did not know about her. That was what he must learn about her before they married, and he realized learning it would involve a very painful brand of humility on his part—no way around that.

Before they left, Magdalene Mullins said, "I was prompted to grab you a clean shirt and underwear before we rushed out of the house. Do you want them?"

"Mom, you're amazing," he exclaimed, "Teddy pooped this disgusting black, sticky stuff all down my front. I could really use a clean shirt," He said as he pulled his damp, green polo shirt away from his belly.

His mother laughed as she dug around in her notoriously over-sized shoulder bag. She pulled out an identical polo shirt, only in navy. "Having nine children redefines the phrase 'traveling light,' she always said." Ted gratefully accepted his clean shirt.

"I wonder when you'll be coming home," mused James Mullins.

Ted said, "Somebody told me to stay with her until she asked me to leave."

Magdalene said, "That was good advice; and you may keep my car until then. I can make do with borrowing."

Ted looked at his parents standing facing him with their arms around one another and said, "You are the most wonderful of parents; I don't deserve you, but I'm very thankful to have you."

They left smiling and thinking an opposite thought, "In spite of all our failures, we have a son that we have not earned. His character is a gracious answer to prayer, rather than a product of our great parenting."

When Ted returned to Jill and Teddy's room, they were in the center of a ring of enthusiastic loved ones. And yet as he walked up to the bed, he saw relief in Jill's face. All she said was, "I'm glad you didn't leave."

Ted just smiled and said, "I'll go as soon as you are tired and need my exit, but you're stuck with me until then."

Mrs. Kelly said, "She is getting tired, Ted. And perhaps that is why you should stay. Holly and I must pack up their things and get out of the dormitory tonight. Megan must go to work in the morning. Sanora says that if Jill and Teddy have a good night, I can take them home in the morning. If you can help them tonight, Holly, Megan, and I, not to mention my men at home, will help her the rest of the summer. Holly and I have reserved a room in the Holiday Inn Express, not a quarter mile from here. We could spell you if things aren't going well. Are you free tonight?"

"He looked at Jill and simply asked, Me?"

"Please, Ted," she urged. "I want Teddy to spend as much time with you as possible, and . . . me too. I'll need to leave you in the morning."

Then Sanora entered the discussion; "The hospital wheels in another bed for the father. And we bring dinner for both of you."

Ted weakly added, "But isn't that the problem? . . . I'm not the father."

Sanora smiled and said, "I'm a great one for defining terms. In my line of work, the term 'father' often needs defining. I do it according to this distinction. The first type I call a 'biological father,' and this father is defined merely by a genetic contribution. The second type I call a 'functional father,' and he is defined by doing what a father ought to do. I often see little connection between the two types of fathers. You may not be of the first type, but I assure you that you have already excelled in the second. In a functional sense, you are this baby's father."

It occurred to Ted then for the first time that Sanora must have heard him talking to Jill about his desire for her—Funny how he could have been unaware of somebody else at a moment like that. All he said was, "I'd love to help Jill tonight."

Mrs. Kelly left with Holly and a kiss for each of them, including Ted. Megan said, "I just hate to leave. But if I don't keep my job this summer, I'll need to work during semester, and then I couldn't babysit. I've got to hit the trail to Concord."

Jill smiled contentedly and said, "We'll be just fine. See you soon."

As Megan scampered away, a nurse rolled a bed in and parked it beside Jill's bed. The warmed bassinet was parked on the other side of Jill's bed. Ted pulled the rocking chair up on that side.

Soon another nurse appeared with two special hospital dinners. There was even a bottle of champagne on ice. The nurse said, "Our cafeteria often earns the epithet, 'hospital food,' but for the first night with a new baby, they go all out. Congratulations you two."

A few minutes later, Teddy fell asleep at the breast. Ted picked him up and laid him in the bassinet, and they enjoyed a darn good steak dinner together, mightily entertained by watching Teddy sleep. After dinner they prayed together, and then Ted popped the cork on the champagne. When he did, Teddy's little fisted arms flew out, but he didn't wake up. Ted

Chapter 24

smilingly said, "Good thing she didn't ask for our ID, when she brought in the champagne."

After her glass was emptied, Jill positively crashed. She fell so soundly asleep that to wake her seemed impossible. Ted began to wilt himself, and lay down on his own bed. It seemed he had just fallen asleep, when he started awake by Teddy's howling. He handed him to Jill, and lay back down. In a few moments he heard another rumble emanate from Teddy's bottom. Between breasts, Ted changed his diaper. A similar process repeated itself every couple hours throughout that dreamlike night. The light on the changing table had a dimmer that Ted left low all night. They were a team, working together in the near dark. They were together, and they loved one another. They were very tired, but very joyful.

Throughout the next three years, they remembered that night and longed to be together through every night. It was the only night they spent together before their wedding.

Epilogue

Let thy fountain be blessed: and rejoice with the wife of thy youth.

—Proverbs 5:18

On June 23 of 2017 Nora and Luke attended a beautiful, garden wedding and adoption ceremony on Mullins Mountain. The Rev. Dr. Cormac Bruce officiated. He had written the recommendation for the groom's tuition scholarship at his alma mater. Ted had recently graduated from Regent's Park College, Oxford, and would soon begin work on a PhD in theology at St. Mary's College, St. Andrews. He hoped to become an Anglican priest. The bride had recently graduated from Blue Ridge State University and would soon begin as an interior designer for Muir, Walker & Pride. She would be working around childcare out of their future flat in Fife. While her new husband had earned his merit scholarship, she would earn the money for their living expenses. Without her job, Ted would not have been able to accept the scholarship, for the program was too intensive to work and study. For the time being, she would support him financially.

The ring-bearer was a bright, happy, handsome three-year-old, the spitting image of his mother. He proudly informed the Shaws at the reception that, "Now my name is Theodore Mullins, and I have a daddy."

Bibliography

Chesterton, G. K. *The Universe according to G. K. Chesterton: A Dictionary of the Mad, Mundane and Metaphysical*. New York: Dover, 2011.
Crabb, Larry. *Fully Alive: A Biblical Vision of Gender That Frees Men and Women to Live beyond Stereotypes*. Grand Rapids: Baker, 2013.
Dubrow, Heather. *Genre*. London: Methuen, 1982.
Erdemgil, Selahattin. *Ephesus*. Translated by Nuket Eraslan. Istanbul: Turistik Yayinlari, 1986.
Guinness, Os. *The Case for Civility: And Why Our Future Depends on It*. New York: HarperOne, 2008.
Hunt, Keith, and Gladys M. Hunt. *For Christ and the University: The Story of InterVarsity Christian Fellowship*. Downers Grove: InterVarsity, 1991.
Longman, Tremper, III. *How to Read the Psalms*. Downers Grove: IVP Academic, 1988.
Nicole, Roger. "Biblical Egalitarianism and the Inerrancy of Scripture." *Priscilla Papers* 20.2 (2006) 4–9.
———. *Standing Forth: Collected Writings of Roger Nicole*. Fearn: Christian Focus, 2002.
Pierce, Ronald W., and Rebecca Merrill Groothuis, eds. *Discovering Biblical Equality: Complementarity without Hierarchy*. Downers Grove: InterVarsity, 2004.
Sayers, Dorothy L. *Are Women Human?* Grand Rapids: Eerdmans, 2005.
Schaff, Philip, and Henry Wace, eds. *Select Library of Nicene and Post-Nicene Fathers I*. Peabody, MA: Hendricksen, 1994.
Tolkien, J. R. R. *The Hobbit*. Boston: Houghton Mifflin, 1997.
Waltke, Bruce K. *An Old Testament Theology*. Grand Rapids: Zondervan, 2007.
Herbert, George. *The English Poems of George Herbert*. Edited by Helen Wilcox. Cambridge: Cambridge University Press, 2007.
Wollstonecraft, Mary. *A Vindication of the Rights of Woman*. New York: Dover, 1996.

www.ingramcontent.com/pod-product-compliance
Lightning Source LLC
Chambersburg PA
CBHW071504150426
43191CB00009B/1415